Happy are those who know they are spiritually poor;

   the Kingdom of heaven belongs to them!

Happy are those who mourn;

   God will comfort them!

Happy are those who are humble;

   they will receive what God has promised!

*Happy are those whose greatest desire
is to do what God requires;*

   God will satisfy them fully!

Happy are those who are merciful to others;

   God will be merciful to them!

Happy are the pure in heart;

   they will see God!

Happy are those who work for peace;

   God will call them his children!

*Happy are those who are persecuted
because they do what God requires;*

   the Kingdom of heaven belongs to them!

MATTHEW 5:3-10 *(Good News Translation)*

an incomplete guide
to the rest
of your Life

Stan D. Gaede

on the road to meaning, purpose & happiness

InterVarsity Press
Downers Grove, Illinois

InterVarsity Press
P.O. Box 1400, Downers Grove, IL 60515-1426
World Wide Web: www.ivpress.com
E-mail: mail@ivpress.com

InterVarsity Press® *is the book-publishing division of InterVarsity Christian Fellowship/USA*®*, a student movement active on campus at hundreds of universities, colleges and schools of nursing in the United States of America, and a member movement of the International Fellowship of Evangelical Students. For information about local and regional activities, write Public Relations Dept., InterVarsity Christian Fellowship/USA, 6400 Schroeder Rd., P.O. Box 7895, Madison, WI 53707-7895, or visit the IVCF website at* <www.ivcf.org>.

Chapter fourteen is a condensed version of the first chapter of Surprised by God, *published by Zondervan in 1993.*

Cover photograph: Alexander Stewart/Image Bank
ISBN 0-8308-2313-1
Printed in the United States of America ∞

Library of Congress Cataloging-in-Publication Data

Gaede, S. D.
    An incomplete guide to the rest of your life: on the road to meaning, purpose &
    happiness/Stan D. Gaede.
       p. cm
    ISBN 0-8308-2313-1 (paper: alk. paper)
    1. Happiness—Religious aspects—Christianity. 2. Christian life. I. Title.
    BV4647.J68 G34 2002
    248.4—dc21   *2001051568*

19	18	17	16	15	14	13	12	11	10	9	8	7	6	5	4	3	2	1
18	17	16	15	14	13	12	11	10	09	08	07	06	05	04	03	02		

For Kirsten,
because love has a good memory

contents

part 1: a deeper love

part 2: a fuller joy

part 3: a Lasting peace

Acknowledgments

The more one writes, the more impossible these things become. Too much indebtedness, too little space. Suffice it to say, the people that have enabled this effort are legion. First and foremost among them are my wife and family, who continue to be my teachers as well as the fodder for my tales; to them I am grateful and apologetic at the same time. Running a close second would be my students, whose questions continue to provoke my learning, and whose lives inspire my own; what a gift you are. This manuscript would not have taken shape, moreover, without the help of Connie Gundry Tappy, whose encouragement and editorial eye made this endeavor possible; for her multiple talents and her friendship I am grateful. Finally, I am the product of two extraordinary communities: Westmont College, where I became a learner in the first place and where I now serve; and Gordon College, where I taught for many years; my debt to both is incalculable, my affection without restraint. What can you say about such friends!

Introduction

Happiness and how to find it: that is the question. If anything has characterized the human condition, it is the search for personal joy and fulfillment. And that seems especially true of late. Indeed, over the last decade we seem to have plunged headlong into a search for happiness, with our celebrities, politicians and heroes leading the way.

And, as if on cue, our culture provided us with lots of options. Relationships, first and foremost. If you've got the right friends or companions, we assumed, you can be happy. Experiences, however, seemed to be a popular second choice, whether the experience involved travel or worship, sex or drugs. We wanted to experience things. Together. And often. To that end, we pursued advanced degrees and better jobs. That we might have the resources to find the best friends, with whom to have the best time. And be happy.

But disappointments and detours keep mucking up our quest.

People fail us. Jobs don't materialize or don't satisfy. And world events keep undermining our sense of composure. Despite the hunt, in other words, satisfaction seems to elude us at every turn. And the question is, why? Why is happiness so elusive, even if we have the time and resources to pursue it?

Make no mistake: Happiness is the right ambition. Jesus assumes it in his teaching from beginning to end. And it is born out in our deepest longings. The question isn't, should we be happy? It's how? It is not a question to be avoided, therefore, but pursued. Indeed, for the Christian, at the beginning of his or her career, it is the question of a lifetime.

At its core, this is a book about the pursuit of happiness. It is rooted in my own quest, to be sure, but it is loaded with questions from others who have helped me along the way. It begins with two assumptions which will go uncontested. The first I have already mentioned: that happiness is worth pursuing. Our problem, I believe, is not that we value happiness too much, but too little.

Second, I am assuming, as well, that this pursuit has something to do with *love* and *joy* and *peace*. That conviction no doubt stems from my faith. But, curiously enough, when you scratch around below the surface, most people seem to agree. The question isn't their relationship to happiness; it's their discovery. What is love, anyway, and to whom do I give it? Where is joy precisely, and how will I find it? And what and where is peace? And how in the world can I experience it?

Those are the guiding questions in our journey. And herein lie a few glimpses from one pilgrim's pursuit.

1

ON Love & NeiGHBOR

(Passing a Bum)

During Christmas vacation, I got up early one morning and, while working on the coffee, noticed a note on the kitchen counter. "LOVE DAD $100," it seemed to say. I could tell from the scrawl that this was from our youngest daughter, Kirsten. Actually, I couldn't tell that immediately, since all of the women in our family have the same handwriting. It's the most amazing thing. The men write one way—call it neo-illegible—and the women write in another—much more rounded, elegant and generally more readable.

Anyway, I could tell this was from the elegant side of the family. But it was also done in a very rushed fashion, which made it a little less elegant than normal, and a little less readable. I quickly assessed the situation and determined that this must be from my seventeen-year-old daughter. That's because our oldest daughter lives in Palo Alto, and the only other female resident in the house, my wife, rarely calls me "dad." Besides, she loves me more than $100.

Now the next significant thing I had to do was figure out what exactly it meant. The coffee was still brewing, so I wasn't thinking all that clearly yet. My first thought was that she was attempting to ascribe some worth to our relationship. The old man is worth about a hundred dollars to me. That was a possibility. But it seemed a little high. I mean, a teenager can do a lot with a hundred dollars these days. Buy a CD, perhaps. Or make a down payment on . . . virtually nothing. Anyway, I couldn't quite figure it out. But it was the Christmas season. Perhaps she was feeling generous.

As I pondered the note, however, I began having additional questions. Why did she leave it out on the counter, for example? Did she want me to see it? Was this some kind of love note? Or was this just a reminder to herself? You know, "No matter what ridiculous thing Dad does, I still must remember that I love him a hundred dollars."

I poured my first cup of coffee, hoping to get more clarity on the subject. Nothing happened. But all the conjuring over money so early in the morning reminded me that I needed to go down to the bank to cover a few bills and also take out a little Christmas cash. I quickly went over to my desk, figured out my fast-developing Christmas debts and jumped into the car to take a ride down to the bank.

The bank wasn't open, of course, but the ATM—a modern invention I employ with great regularity and delight—was. I haven't talked to a teller in years. Not even sure they still exist. Anyway, after carrying on a deeply meaningful conversation with the ATM, I jumped back into my car and left the parking lot. Not far down the road, I came to a stop sign—not too unusual, I know—but this one's worth mentioning because of what was sitting directly under it: a bum, as we used to say (until that word was co-opted for purposes of anatomical description).

A person, in other words, in his thirties or forties, with a beard nicely trimmed. Old clothes nicely cleaned. A kind face nicely graced with a smile. And a sign nicely displaying this rather straightforward but haunting message: AM HUNGRY! WILL WORK FOR FOOD.

I read the sign fairly quickly, and then glanced up at the fellow's eyes, hoping not to meet them, but knowing I couldn't keep from extending the courtesy. Sure enough, his eyes were there, big as potatoes, looking at mine, and looking equally as nice as everything else about him. "Phooey," I said to myself. "Now what do I do?" It was a four-way boulevard stop, with four cars each awaiting their turn, and my turn coming up . . . not quickly enough. I pulled my eyes back to business, watching the other cars with some intensity, and calculating that I had about five seconds before it was my turn to hit the accelerator.

"Not enough time to reach for my billfold," was the first thought that came to mind. Better keep moving along. Besides, the fellow wants work, not money. And I've got nothing to offer him. "Better keep moving along," I repeated to myself. "Five, four, three, two . . ." Hours have moved more quickly than those five seconds. Finally, it was my turn to hit the gas. And I did so. Like a bat out of hell, to be honest with you. Which is pretty much the place I thought I was escaping from. Or moving toward. I wasn't sure which.

I hit the play button on my tape deck. "This moment calls for a little diversion," I thought. *"Away in a manger no crib for his bed; the little Lord Jesus . . ."* Wham! I hit the button again, suddenly preferring silence to Christmas. "Am hungry; will work for food," was what I heard instead. And it was the thing I kept hearing for the next ten minutes, until I stepped across the threshold of my door and into my home.

Fortunately, my daughter, the teenager, was now occupying

the kitchen, grabbing her cereal of choice and staking her claim on the morning newspaper. "Morning, Hon," I said, my gloom disappearing in an instant as I heard my cereal-crunching teenager respond, "Morning, Dad." You have no idea what those two words mean to me, by the way. In the first place, I don't always hear them. I'm up pretty early most mornings, and sometimes we just don't see each other. But some mornings we don't want to, both of us being on the grumpy side anytime before noon.

Suddenly I spied the note on the counter, which I had noticed while making coffee. "Hon," I said, placing the note on the table, just under the chin of my now paper-reading daughter. "What does this mean? LOVE DAD $100." Kirsten suddenly burst out laughing, barely catching herself to keep from spraying the entire kitchen with cereal. She swallowed hard. "Dad, you dork! It says, 'I OWE DAD $100.' Remember, I ran short on money for Christmas presents, and so you loaned me a hundred dollars. This was just a note to remind me to pay you back."

She looked at me with that "I love you even though you're a little slow" look, and I could tell she meant no harm. But it was still a blow, to be honest with you. First of all, it wasn't that dumb of a mistake. She was the one that put the "I" so close to the "O" that it looked like *love* in the first place. Besides, I had just learned that what I thought was some form of weird teenage love note was in fact an IOU. I had not only lost a little love, but I was reminded of the fact that I had lost a little money as well. Things were not going well.

I must have looked crestfallen because Kirsten quickly intervened. "Oh Dad, you big goofball. Don't you know I love you a lot more than $100? At least $150," she added with a smile. And then she coupled it with a hug. "Besides, Dad," she said, "the

IOU *is* a love note. You loaned me the money out of love; I'm paying you back for the same reason. Love has a good memory, you know."

She quickly went back to her newspaper and her cereal. But I . . . did not. Instead, I got back in my car and drove back to the corner near the bank. Back to the fellow standing under the stop sign who was still there, with the same smile and the same sign. When I reached the stop, I caught his eyes again, thought about my daughter's comment (love has a good memory) and handed him something. It's not important what, or how much. Just something that seemed appropriate, given what I had available that day. And given what I owed.

"Thank you very much," he said, "Merry Christmas."

"Same to you," I said, just a little choked. "Same to you."

The Cost of Love
So, why did I do that? And more to the point, what do you do when you pass someone on the road who wants your assistance? That's the question. And it's a question I have asked, and been asked, all of my life. I have been asked it because, for many years, I taught a course on social stratification, where status and class differences were discussed at length, and where questions like this came up all the time.

And I have asked it personally because like the rest of you, I have often come across people, right in my path, who have desired my help. Sometimes it's just a tin can in someone's hand, asking for change for a cup of coffee. Sometimes it's a person with a sign providing a bit more detail: I'm an unemployed vet. Or I'm homeless. Or I'm looking for work. Or any number of other messages, all designed to make a case and make me reach into my pocket and provide them with a bit of help.

And you haven't a clue what they're going to do with the money, do you? Not a clue. They could take it and spend it on alcohol. That's a very real possibility, by the way, if the research I have seen is accurate. Or they could spend it on bread and cheese. Or clothing. Or a ticket to get them back home, for that matter. There are any number of possibilities. And as you stand there trying to figure out what in the world to do with your hard-earned cash, you must contemplate the fact that your money—if you give it to them—could be used for good or for ill. So what do you do?

One passage that frequently comes to mind in times like this is the story of the Good Samaritan. It's worth a read:

On one occasion an expert in the law stood up to test Jesus. "Teacher," he asked, "what must I do to inherit eternal life?"

"What is written in the Law?" he replied. "How do you read it?"

He answered: " 'Love the Lord your God with all your heart and with all your soul and with all your strength and with all your mind'; and 'love your neighbor as yourself.' "

"You have answered correctly," Jesus replied. "Do this and you will live."

But he wanted to justify himself, so he asked Jesus, "And who is my neighbor?"

In reply Jesus said: "A man was going down from Jerusalem to Jericho, when he fell into the hands of robbers. They stripped him of his clothes, beat him and went away, leaving him half dead. A priest happened to be going down the same road, and when he saw the man, he passed by on the other side. So too, a Levite, when he came to the place and saw him, passed by on the other side. But a Samaritan, as he traveled, came where the man was; and when he saw him, he took pity on him. He went to him and bandaged his wounds, pouring on oil and wine. Then he put the man on his own donkey, took him to an inn and took care of him. The next day he took out two silver coins and gave them to the innkeeper. 'Look after him,' he said, 'and when I return, I will reimburse you for any extra expense you may have.'

"Which of these three do you think was a neighbor to the man who fell into the hands of robbers?"

The expert in the law replied, "The one who had mercy on him."

Jesus told him, "Go and do likewise." (Luke 10:25-37)

At first glance, Jesus doesn't seem to be all that helpful in answering our question, right? After all, the story that Jesus told of the good Samaritan is far more clear-cut than the situation I encountered. The man in trouble in the parable is not sitting on a corner with a sign, asking for help. Rather, according to Jesus, he was robbed and left stripped and beaten on the side of the road. He clearly was in need. The priest and the Levite, for whatever reason, ignored that need. The Samaritan did not. He saw the need and responded in kindness and mercy. It was not easy, this kindness he provided. It cost him two days' wages, plus a great deal of time; the Samaritan was extremely generous with mercy, in other words. But at least he knew he was helping a victim—someone who truly needed his help.

But we generally don't know that, do we? I see someone on the street asking for money, and I don't have any idea if that person is the victim, or if I am. Are they being honest, or are they being shrewd? Am I being generous if I give them something, or am I being stupid? You see, I know what to do when I see someone lying half dead on the side of the road. But what am I supposed to do about those who are alive and smiling, with a sign that says, "AM HUNGRY! WILL WORK FOR FOOD"?

My dad had an answer to this dilemma, by the way. He offered them a job. He could do that because he owned a farm, and there was always work to be done on a farm. And so whenever he encountered someone who was needy and asking for food, he always did two things: First, he would give them a bit of cash to hold them over. And second, he'd give them a card with his name on it, along with his address and phone number, and tell them to meet him at 6:00 the next morning. "I'll find work for you," he'd say.

The interesting thing was, sometimes they showed up, and sometimes they didn't. And those who did show up would usually work for just a day or so, or in some cases, a week. In a few cases, they became long-term employees. One worked for my dad until my father died many years later. And when I think about him, and I think about my dad, it sends chills down my spine. He was a wonderful man. A better worker I've never seen. He just needed a helping hand, and my father was there to give it to him. As a result, my father got much more in return than he ever gave or ever bargained for.

You just don't know, do you? And no one does know. That included the priest and the Levite in the parable, as well as the good Samaritan. As well as my father. You see, I don't think any of them had any idea what their help, or lack thereof, would accomplish. And I think that's almost always the case.

Look, the road from Jericho to Jerusalem—which Jesus was probably thinking about in his parable—was a seventeen-mile hike. It was rough and rocky and dangerous. If you came across a man lying on the side of the road, you would have all kinds of questions. The first would probably be about your own safety in such a situation. But the second would be about the victim, if that's what he really was. You might ask why this fellow is traveling alone in such territory anyway. And is he really a victim, or part of a gang of thugs? The one who was left behind perhaps? Or maybe he's a stooge, pretending to be hurt, only to lure you in to be accosted by other robbers lying in wait when you stop to give assistance. The possibilities are endless, as are the reasons not to help. Which is probably why the priest and the Levite did not.

But the good Samaritan did, with all the same questions in front of him, plus perhaps a few more. The Jews considered Samaritans ethnically and spiritually inferior to the Jews, remember. I don't know if the victim was a Jew or not, but he could have been. Whatever barriers he crossed to offer help, however, the good Samaritan clearly paid a price for his hospitality. He took a risk in the first place, a risk avoided by the priest and Levite. He took his time, in the second; time which surely could have been used for more self-serving ventures. And finally he took his money—his own money—and paid for the fellow's lodging, and even offered to cover additional expenses in the future, if such were needed. This was an extravagant mercy, in other words, aimed at a man he didn't know and offered without any knowledge or assurance of the result.

This was true of my father as well, by the way, when he offered his name and address and a job to strangers who might be in need. You see, it's easy for me to say, looking back, "Oh well, Dad had a farm. He had jobs to offer. I do not." What I forget is that you don't operate a business that way. You hire only when you have a need, and you hire the best person for the job. Anything less is bad practice. What I forget is that he offered his name and address to a complete stranger, at some risk to himself and his family—who also lived at that address. What I forget is that he invested quite a bit of time in people who never showed up, or showed up for just a few hours, or showed up and worked so poorly that someone else had to come along and straighten out everything they did a few hours later. What I forget is that the rest of us also lived on farms. And we just walked right by.

Which brings me again to my decision to go back and give that fellow a little something: Why did I do that? Well, the short answer is, because it was the least I could do, under the circumstances. It wasn't the right thing to do, in any ethical sense, by the way. Nor is it something I would encourage others to do necessarily. My action that day was filled with too much ignorance, too much uncertainty, too much gray, to inflict it on anyone else. But it was the right thing for me to do. And I figured that out while talking to Kirsten that morning about her debt.

Why did I loan Kirsten a hundred dollars to buy Christmas presents anyway? Because she asked me, that's why. Now, I must tell you, I don't give Kirsten everything she wants. She's very familiar with phrases like "No way," "Not a chance," "Not on your life," "Nada." But whether I say yes or no, I do it for one reason: because I love her. Love her like you can't imagine. Love her so much it makes my heart ache just thinking about it. And when she said she had a few more presents she wanted to buy but had depleted her own resources, I was more than happy to step up to the plate and give her a bridge loan; to help her out until she could pay me back. I thought it was a good cause, to a good daughter, whom I love a bunch.

And that's why she wrote me the "LOVE DAD $100" note; or, as it was actually written, "I OWE DAD $100." *Love has a good memory* was the way she put it that day. She didn't want to forget what she owed me. And she didn't want me to forget either. She called it a love note, and that's a pretty accurate description, I think. It was a reminder of our mutual trust and mutual responsibility because of our mutual love for one another.

And that takes me to the man standing on the street corner.

Why did I return to give him a few dollars? Because love has a
good memory. It remembers that nothing I have is of my own
doing. That all I have or am or ever will be is the gift of my Creator, my Lord and my God. There are no self-made men or
women on this planet. They don't exist. There are only God-
created people, each one an act of creative genius, all master-
pieces in their own right. And God loves them all, if I read my
Bible correctly. Every one of them. Loves them more than I love
my daughter. Aches for them. Longs for them to know him, to
be reconciled to him, to become the people he created them to
be in the first place. Which is why he sent Jesus: born to die so
that we might live; born to pay for our sin, that we might be reconciled to a sinless, holy God.

Who Is Your Neighbor?

Costly business, this salvation. Costly. And unfair. And totally
undeserved. Sort of like the life God gave us in the first place.
Which may have been why Jesus said, "whatever you did for
one of the least of these, . . . you did for me (Matthew 25:40)."
Because doing for those who can't do for themselves is Jesus'
business; it's God work. Why? Because it's a modest replica-
tion—a very poor imitation of what God does for us all the time.
All the time. He gives, and we receive. That's the deal. Which
means he gives, and we owe. Big time. Every day we write IOUs,
one right after the other, and think almost nothing of it. God's
kitchen counter is littered with IOU notes; and they all have our
names on them.

   Who is my neighbor? That was the question that Jesus was
answering when he told the story of the good Samaritan. This
wasn't a lesson on social ethics, though I think it has ethical
implications. Nor was it a lesson on how to care for the needy. It
was a lesson on truth. The Pharisees listening to Jesus that day

knew the command: Love God and love your neighbor. But one smart aleck asked, "But . . . but . . . Jesus, who *is* my neighbor, anyway?" You have to picture him with a knowing smile on his face, knowing that he had asked the impossible question. Knowing that you can't love everyone equally. "You've got to make choices, Jesus, about where to spend your time. So, Jesus, if you're so smart: Whom do I choose to love? Who is my neighbor?"

And Jesus says, "You don't choose, my smiling friend. I choose. Your neighbor is anyone who comes across your path who has a need. Anyone. Why? Because the Lord God created them all. Loves them all, every bit as much as he loves you. Cannot you, who have been given so much, do a little? Can't you, with so many IOUs on God's kitchen counter, give without receiving once in a while? Give without knowing the consequences of your giving?"

And that seemed to me to be a pretty good question. Which is why, on that day with my daughter, in my own kitchen, this Pharisee said, "Yes, Jesus, I can." Which is why I got back in my car and gave a little to a man who is loved a lot. A man who cannot repay me. Who doesn't know me from Adam. But is of Adam. Who may indeed squander what I have given him, and thereby replicate the way I squander God's gifts to me almost every day. But who will, at least for a moment, see Jesus in action, whether he knows it or not. And so will I.

"Whatever you did for one of the least of these, . . . you did for me."

2

ON Love & faithfuLNess

(Being There)

Dr. Gaede, what are you thankful for this Thanksgiving?" It came out of the blue, this question. And not with large intent. In fact, what happened was that I was walking from my office toward the Dining Commons with two students, who just happened to get stuck with me on their way to lunch. One uttered an obligatory "Hi," and I responded with the expected "Hello. How are you?" "Fine," he said, with a smile and a lie. And then I asked cleverly, "On your way to lunch?" Which we all knew was a stupid question, because the DC is the only place anyone is going at that time of the day. "Yeah," came his polite response, no doubt covering feelings of complete incredulity.

After that, silence set in—both of us probably wondering whether we could make it to the DC without saying anything else. And then, bless him, he remembered that he was a Christian and thought, "Hey, the president needs some help here. Let me see, what can I say that might put him at ease? I know, I'll ask him about Thanksgiving. That's right around the cor-

ner." And so he said, "Dr. Gaede, what are you thankful for this
Thanksgiving?" And I looked at him with more than a little surprise, but more than a little gratefulness as well. Because, in the
first place, I knew the intent of his heart. But more than that, I
knew I had just heard the topic for my chapel talk the next
Monday.

Why? Well, because this particular Thanksgiving was going to
be just a little different for me. It was to be the first Thanksgiving of my entire life without my mom. Not that she had always
been with us at table, of course. Over the previous few decades,
we were often separated by distance at Thanksgiving, she being
a Californian and we having moved to New England right after
graduate school. So we weren't always nibbling on the same
drumstick. But she was always there in spirit whether she was
there in body or not. And I pretty much took that for granted.

But I didn't that Thanksgiving, because just a few months
earlier, on August 11, only one day before her eighty-fourth
birthday, Evelyn Sarah Gaede said goodbye to us . . . and good
morning to her Savior. It was a good move on her part because
she had been bedridden for months and was a long way from
the woman we had known and loved for nearly eighty-four
years. Nevertheless, I missed her. A lot. Still do.

Remembering Mom
Quite a few years back, I began using the early morning hour of
each day for prayer. I pray about lots of things—family, friends,
needs, blessings—and I do it in something of an order. There
was always a place in my prayers for my mom—a time when I
would lift her up and ask the Lord to take care of her. Keep her
safe. And sometimes, keep her ignorant of what I was up to!

But all of a sudden, after all those years of regularly praying
for my mom, when I got to that point in my prayers, when it was

her turn . . . well, what to say? It just kind of brought me up short. It still does. And so I stop. And wonder. And wonder some more. How could it be? How could my life with my mom, as well as my dad, be over? Already? It just doesn't seem possible. And then I do the only thing I can do, after the wonderment, which is to give thanks to the God who gave me my mom and dad in the first place. Because they were gifts. And because I am grateful.

I wasn't always, however, and that's part of the story as well. Our lives with our parents are always complicated, aren't they? That was certainly the case for me. If you've ever read anything else I've written, you might know that I tell stories about my father all the time. And for good reason. My dad was an amazing man, whom I looked up to from day one, who almost never failed me, and who was a model of integrity and wisdom and intelligence. Dad was not perfect, to be sure. But with every bone in my body, I admired my dad deeply—as did almost everyone else who knew him. And I never doubted for a moment whom I wanted to be like when I grew up. Nor how far I had to go to get there.

But with my mom it was different. Growing up, I never considered her to be someone I ought to emulate. And I suspect that was true for my sister and brother as well. I loved Mom, but I didn't entirely admire her in those early years. Why? Well, if you had asked me then, I would have probably said that mom thought too much about herself. And she didn't keep her thoughts hidden either. When she was uncomfortable, everyone knew about it. When she was hungry, we all got the word. When she was tired, we all got a little sleepy. Mom was not the least bit hesitant to let us know about her needs.

One of my keenest memories of my mom, for example, was her rather intimate relationship with the thermostat in our home. She was at that thing twenty-four hours a day, turning it up a little bit if she was cold, turning it down just a tad if she was hot, and never, never, never trusting anyone else even to go near it. I mean, she *owned* it. And you were in the deepest of trouble if you even looked at, much less adjusted, the temperature.

Nor did I think of my mom as being particularly wise. I don't mean, by the way, that my mom was unintelligent. I think she was quite bright, actually—a good student through high school and college. But she wasn't really curious about the world as a whole, and especially not about anything of a political or cultural or historical nature.

I remember in the years right after my father's death, my mom decided to do a bit of traveling, which was absolutely the right thing for her to do. She had both the time and the means for such ventures, and so we, her children, encouraged her to see the world. Which she did. The problem was, she didn't really *learn* anything about the world from her travels.

She'd visit the pyramids in Egypt and when she came home, all she could do was talk about the person she met on the camel beside her. She'd fly off to Rome or Paris and return with picture after picture of people and places, hardly remembering anything about their historical significance but able to share in detail about how she was feeling that day—whether she was hot or cold, happy or sad. It used to drive me crazy because it seemed to me that she found it very hard to engage the world around her and really become a student. Learning, and reflecting on what you have learned, was and is as important to me as anything one can do. And sometimes Mom wouldn't do it.

And so Mom frustrated me. She came to conclusions I didn't especially like. She approached life in ways that made me wince. Especially during my years as a teenager, I had a hard time respecting her. She didn't measure up to my standards.

That view of my mom began to change, however, when I was nineteen years old. That was when I was involved in a car accident and wound up spending two months in a hospital, then five months flat on my back in a hospital bed in the family room of our home. Because of multiple injuries, I was in a full body cast and totally immobilized. And because my mouth was wired shut, I could hardly talk, much less eat. I was helpless as a baby. So my parents had to do everything for me: bathe me, feed me—you name it, they did it. Because my dad was a farmer and gone most of the day, the bulk of this effort was carried on by my mother, who attended me nearly twenty-four hours a day.

Here's what I noticed—and this is the point: She did all this work . . . *gladly*. Without complaint. And without letup for months on end. Indeed, for all practical purposes, she gave up a year of her life to take care of me. And I'm sure she thought nothing of it. This was simply what a mother did in such circumstances. It was her responsibility, from her perspective, so she did it. Faithfully.

It was not the first time she had practiced such faithfulness, nor would it be the last. In fact, in hindsight, it is now clear to me that my accident was simply the first in a whole string of painful experiences that she would endure in the years thereafter. I was the youngest of three children, which means that, at the time of my accident, she came within a hair's breadth of losing her youngest child; I almost died. While I was still recuperating from the accident, moreover, her oldest child, my brother, became very ill—only a year after having completed his Ph.D. in chemistry and settling with his family in a fine place and at a fine university. And because of his illness, she had to watch him give up the job he'd worked so hard for and the life he had planned. A few years after that, her husband, my father—who was without doubt the love of her life and her security as well—

was diagnosed with a brain tumor. She lost him just two years after the diagnosis. Not too many years after that, she walked with her daughter, my sister, through the dissolution of a marriage and, because of it, the breakup of the family farm.

Looking back now, I am struck by both the severity and the "piling on" nature of those calamities. They came one right after the other. And they were heavy blows—especially when you consider that, prior to that time, my mom had lived something of a charmed life. She came from a very close family, full of security and warmth; though poor, they were rich in relationships. That pattern continued in her early adult years after she married my father, only this time she managed to find prosperity in economy as well as relationships, since my dad did reasonably well as a farmer. And so, just before my accident, things were going pretty well for my mom. Life was good, and Mom felt blessed.

But in the next decade, all of that changed. Almost all of it. And what was Mom's response? Surprise. Disappointment. And lots of tears. But almost no anger. And absolutely no retreat—no retreat from continuing to do the things that needed to be done, out of faithfulness to God and those whom God had given her.

Lessons Learned

Now, as I think back on all of this, two things strike me in particular. The first is how dull I was as a youngster in my reflections on my mom—how dull and self-centered and simple-minded. It was bad enough to think my standards were better than hers; but it was selfish and downright arrogant to think that she ought to measure up on my yardstick. I was a fool in wise clothing.

But the second thing that strikes me now—and the one that's more relevant perhaps—is how difficult it is these days for us to appreciate people who are simply faithful and responsible. People who are just doing what they *ought* to do. You see, for years and years, I was critical of my mom for not being a certain kind of person—for not being the insightful, perceptive person that I wanted her to be. And as a result, I missed precisely the person she was—the gift she was to me and to the rest of my family. I failed to appreciate what I had, in other words, because I was hoping for something I had not. The odd thing is, I already had most of those other qualities in my dad, which means the Lord had already given me one parent who had the qualities I so prized. Why then wasn't I satisfied? Why didn't I just thank God for the one, and then for the other, and realize that I was twice blessed?

Part of the answer, clearly, has to do with me, and my own limitations and weaknesses as a young man, growing up in a privileged world. A personal failing, in other words. But the other reality concerns the world in which we find ourselves. To be blunt: we do not find it easy to value "faithfulness," do we? Especially not in this culture, in these days. And I was a man of my times.

In many ways, faithfulness is simply the value of "being there"—being there when and where you are needed in order to do what has to be done. It is not flashy. It does not lead to material success. It rarely gets lifted up in film or television, because it's not all that observable . . . in the short run, at least. And it's certainly not very exciting. Or even interesting.

Think of your favorite sitcom on television, for example. How many times do you even see, much less appreciate, the person who is simply . . . responsible. And faithful. At best, those characters are mere props; at worst, they're the butt of someone else's joke. Let's face it, "being there" is not valued highly in our fast-paced, image-oriented culture. Being funny is great, even if it comes at the expense of others. Being daring is even better, even if it comes at your own expense, because it's risky and exciting. And being successful, or known, or fulfilled . . . well, there's nothing better or more important. Those are the things we seek, our dreams come true. But "being there" is dull. Who cares?

Until, one day, you find yourself lying on a hospital bed, entombed in a body cast, totally incapacitated and totally dependent. And you discover that being daring is stupid. And being great means nothing. But "being there" is everything. Everything you need.

Well, that was me at age nineteen. And suddenly my mom's inability to be insightful or clever or articulate was of no consequence to me at all. But "being there"—something she had been *doing* all my life, and which she continued to do regardless of the circumstances—was incalculable. Immeasurable. More valuable than diamonds and rubies.

The Power of Faithful Parenting
Have you ever wondered why, in the Ten Commandments, the command to honor your parents is so short—and completely unqualified? Listen to it: "Honor your father and your mother, so that you may live long in the land the LORD your God is giving you." I mean, it doesn't say to honor them if they are wise or insightful. Or honor them when they treat you well. Nor does it seem to take into account that parents are immensely finite and fallen, that they do things poorly, make mistakes, and worse yet, sin. That they treat their children unfairly at times, lose it periodically, and fail in countless other ways—all the ways that human beings are capable of failing, in fact.

Nevertheless, God simply says in this command, "Honor your father and your mother." Period. Why would he do that? I hadn't the foggiest idea growing up. But today, looking back, the reason seems pretty clear: It's because "being there" is of high value to God, even if it isn't to us. And the command to honor your parents is a reminder of that fact—to parents as well as children, I think.

It says to parents, your first responsibility to your children is to "be there"—to be faithful in your role as a parent. Your children won't always appreciate it, and you won't find it easy, since your culture doesn't value it. But that doesn't matter. It's the task I've given you, says the Lord. Do it. Which my mom did.

And it seems to me that this command says almost the same thing to children. Your parents are there to care for you, says the Lord; in doing that, they are doing something very close to my heart—playing a role very close to my own. That's why Jesus instructed you to call me your father, your parent—because your parents are supposed to reflect the same kind of care and love for you that I have for you.

But they won't always do that. They will blow it, sometimes badly. But I ask you to honor them, not because what they *do* is always honorable, but because what they *represent* is honorable. They represent me and my commitment to "be there" for you. Whether they are faithful or not, I will be faithful. Whether they are responsible or not, I will be responsible. You can count on it. And every time they manage to rise above themselves and their culture and actually practice such faithfulness, you can do something else as well: You can rejoice and be thankful. For in them, you have seen me.

Which helps explain another passage that seems quite odd in light of the fifth commandment. It's in Luke 14:26, where Jesus says, "If anyone comes to me and does not hate his father and mother, . . . he cannot be my disciple." Strong language, which on the surface sounds rather uncaring and even inconsistent with the command to honor your parents. But it is not, and as it turns out, it was my mom who taught me this one as well.

I became a Christian—gave my life to Christ—as a young boy. I realize that not everyone who is a Christian can point to a precise moment when he gave his life to Christ, but I can. And it involved my mom. One day, I was just playing in my room—you know, doing little boy things like playing with fire engines, pretending to be important and figuring out ways to annoy my older brother—when my mom came into my room and asked, "Stanley, are you a Christian?" It was an odd question, coming in the middle of fire engines. And so I gave mom the answer I thought she wanted. "Sure, Mom. You bet. Jesus loves me, this I know. What's for dinner?" Bad answer. Her brow furrowed, and she proceeded to sit down on the toy chest that held all of my treasures on earth. This was not a good sign—for my treasures or for me—and she quickly launched into a series of difficult questions, the most difficult being, "Why, dear son, do you think you're a Christian?"

"Oh, Ma, you know. I go to church with you guys. Sunday school. Prayers. All that sort of stuff." Her brow furrowed again, now resembling the Grand Canyon. "Stanley," she said, "going to church doesn't make you a Christian. There's a big difference between going to church and following Christ. Some people are very religious, but they don't know Jesus."

"Whoa," I thought, "she's got me there." And in my mind there flashed the image of a particular fellow in our church who was a regular attender but acted like the Grinch who stole Christmas. "Yeah, Mom . . . you mean . . . you mean like Mr. Jones? He sure doesn't seem to . . ." Mom quickly cut me off. "It's not our place to judge, Stanley. Man looks on the outside, but God looks at the heart. The question isn't about Mr. Jones; the question is about you. Do you know Christ as your personal Savior?"

All of a sudden, all my defenses just melted away. Disappeared. It was like someone snapped her fingers, and I went from being the grand apologist to one who knows, or better yet, who is known. In one moment I was armed and protected. In the next, I was naked as a babe and fully exposed. And the light was unbearable, as was my sin. So I gave it all away—my sin and my heart—to Jesus, and he became my Lord.

Of course, my heart sang, and I rejoiced. But here's what I want you to know: The joy of that moment was not only my own. It was mine, to be sure, and I was so overwhelmed by joy in that moment that I literally went running all over the house, whispering in my dad's ear, and then telling my sister, and my dog—and even my brother—that I knew Jesus. They all rejoiced with me. Including my mom.

That's an interesting thing. My mom rejoiced even though she had led me to Another. In that moment she handed me off both literally and figuratively. She told me, by word and by deed, exactly the same thing Jesus was saying. She said, "I am not your God, nor is your dad, nor are you, nor is anyone else in God's creation. You belong not to me, but to your Creator. He made you. You are his and his alone. And you will have no rest until you find your rest in him." And she was right. And she was faithful. And today I am grateful beyond words.

You see, we don't honor our parents because they are perfect, like God, but because they can, in their role, once in a while point us to God. They can do that by how they act. They can do that by what they say. And they can do that, as did my mom, by faithfully "being there" when needed. When that happens, we ought to rejoice and give thanks, because it's rare. And right. And wonderful in the eyes him who made us, our perfectly faithful God and heavenly Father.

And so, today—belatedly but happily—I am grateful. Grateful

for my parents, in general. But grateful for my mom, in particular. For "being there." And for pointing me, in spite of her imperfections, to the One who is perfect. For hiding herself enough so that I could see through her and beyond her to the only One really worth seeing.

I am also grateful to Jesus for revealing himself to me through my mom. For reminding me of my own imperfections through hers. And thus for reminding me of my need for him. Using her light, in other words, slightly dimmed, to show me a Light far brighter—a Way, a Truth and a Life brilliant beyond my imagination.

3

on Love & mercy

(Why Is Mr. Weinberg Still Living?)

It's the middle of the day. I'm in my office pretending to be important, when a student walks in right on time for her appointment. But just as she does, I get a phone call. Being polite, the student says, "Want me to leave until you're finished with the call, Dr. Gaede?" "Nah," I said. "It'll only take a minute. Please come in, make yourself comfortable. I'll be right with you."

The student, having been raised with good manners, doesn't seem to mind. She picks up a paper lying on the table next to her and begins to read. At first, she probably thinks it's a newspaper, but I notice that it's the *Chronicle of Higher Education,* a weekly journal that covers college and university events, read mostly by presidents and deans who enjoy finding out how much trouble other presidents and deans are having at their institutions. It makes us feel better.

I watch the student out of the corner of my eye, expecting her to put the paper away rather quickly . . . or fall asleep. She does neither. In fact, she is reading very intently and increasingly furrowing her brow. I look away and refocus on the phone conversation, soon forgetting that she is even there. Which is why I wind up spending ten minutes on the phone, not one. And why I am surprised to see her still there when I finally put down the receiver.

I look at her somewhat sheepishly and start to apologize, when all at once she blurts out, "Why isn't Mr. Weinberg dead?" Silence ensues as I try to figure out what in the world she is talking about. She repeats her question, "Why isn't Mr. Weinberg dead?"

It's an interesting moment. Is this a theological question, I think, or a biological one? Does she need to be reminded that none of us knows when we're going to die? Or was this a trick question—you know, stump the president and have a good laugh for the day? Not coming up with the answer to any of those questions, I finally say, "Excuse me. I'm not quite following you. What do you mean?"

"This article," she says, "in this odd newspaper you have here on the table. Have you read it? It's about a conference that was held . . . somewhere . . . on the topic of science and religion. And this science guy—Stephen Weinberg—who doesn't believe in God, says all kinds of very rude things about religion and then basically puts God to the test. Right there at this conference. Listen to this: 'The evidence for any and all miracles is weaker than the evidence for cold fusion,' he says. And then he says this—and this is the part that really gets to me: 'If I'm wrong, why doesn't a flaming sword appear and strike me down in my impiety, and then we'll all know the answer?'

"That's it. And Dr. Gaede, I want to know why the man is still living. I mean, why does God put up with this kind of foolishness, anyway? Why doesn't he just let Mr. Weinberg have it, and then we could all put this issue to rest?"

It was a surprising turn of events, to be sure. But it also struck me, once I got over the shock of the thing, that she was asking a very good question. And a very old question. "How long must your servant wait?" cried the psalmist. "When will you punish my persecutors? . . . It is time for you to act, O LORD; your law is being broken" (Psalm 119:84, 126). And my student's question on this particular occasion was perhaps even better than she knew. For you see, the conference she was reading about was a very high profile event on religion and science sponsored by the American Association for the Advancement of Science and the Templeton Foundation. Everyone was there—big names in science and theology from around the world. And one of the biggest names was Dr. Stephen L. Weinberg, physicist and Nobel laureate. I mean, we're not talking just smart here. We're talking super smart. And super outspoken. And super antagonistic toward religion.

Weinberg believes, for example, that religion is not just wrong, it's an insult to human dignity. A crutch for the weak-minded. While it may have done some good at points, he believes its influence, on balance, has been destructive to society. Indeed, one of science's principal accomplishments, he says, has been to release intellectuals from the need to have religious faith. And then in an attempt to prove his point, he basically said at this conference, "I dare you, God. If you're really out there, send down a flaming sword in the middle of this conference and do me in. Then everyone will know that I was wrong about you."

But that didn't happen. And my student wanted to know why. Why didn't God respond? It would certainly have made life easier, wouldn't it? For God, most definitely. And for us as well. I mean, think of the impact of such a thing: If a famous scientist called on God to strike him down, and then—out of the blue—this flaming sword came down from the sky and bisected him, that would close a few mouths, would it not? Can you imagine the headlines the next day: "God, 1. Mr. Weinberg, 0." Billy Graham could probably hold a crusade the following night and win the whole world to Christ.

Why God Doesn't Strike Him Dead

So why didn't God do it? Why didn't he take Mr. Weinberg's dare? Well, of course, I don't know. And that's perhaps the most important thing that one can say regarding God's actions toward another being. Nevertheless, three ideas come quickly to mind.

Option #1: Maybe it's because Mr. Weinberg is a good physicist, and God likes good physicists. I'm serious. Maybe God likes good scientists—even those who don't believe in him—because, whether they know it or not, by revealing more and more of God's creation, they bring him honor and glory.

If you think I'm off base here, look at the Old Testament. God certainly used the "pagan nations" to accomplish his purposes. For example, he used the brutal Assyrian army to judge the northern kingdom of Israel, which had strayed far from him to worship other gods. Later, he used the Babylonians to punish the southern kingdom of Judah for similar reasons. So why not use Mr. Weinberg as part of his good plan today? If God can use Balaam's donkey to speak the truth, he can certainly use Mr. Weinberg, can he not? And let's face it, there is a sense in which Mr. Weinberg is being a good steward, even though he doesn't know it, simply by using his God-given talent to study physics. That's a very good thing to do.

In fact, this line of reasoning seems so compelling that I might just rest my case right here. Except for one thing: Mr. Weinberg doesn't limit his comments to physics. He also likes to make pronouncements about religion that are philosophical, historical and sociological. And the fact is, when he wanders outside of physics and into these other disciplines, his intelligence rather leaves him. Or more precisely, he pays less attention to the data.

He claims, for example, that religion has been, on the whole, socially destructive, anti-scientific and personally repressive. Thus, he says, one of science's greatest achievements has been to liberate us from religion. Well, that's an interesting claim. But the evidence is not persuasive. Indeed, the evidence appears to show almost precisely the reverse.

I say this cautiously but with some justification. As a sociologist of knowledge and culture, I have spent a large part of my adult life engaging other scholars, both within and outside my discipline, who study religion. And interestingly enough, I can't think of one who would agree with Mr. Weinberg's thesis. Not one. They would all agree that religion can be, and has been, socially destructive at times. But they would also argue that it has proven constructive at other times. In other words, like anything else, religion can be used for good and for evil.

Consider the old canard that religion is the source of most of our wars and conflicts. Well, it is true that many wars have been fought in the name of religion. But one needs to remember that, until a century or two ago, almost everyone on both sides of every war was religious; so it is not surprising at all that religion was, at times, used for evil (in the name of good). It was the weapon of choice. Notice what happens when we move into the twentieth century, however, when for the first time we finally have a substantial number of world leaders that are not religious. Some of them have been reasonably decent people, mind you. But perhaps the most notorious in the twentieth century—Hitler, Stalin, Pol Pot, Mao Zedong—were explicitly anti-religious and thought that the elimination of whole peoples was justified to serve their ends. And what was the result?

Well, the result was that the twentieth century was arguably one of the most systematically cruel in human history. And yet we have a hard time facing this fact, don't we? We use the word "medieval" to signify unusual barbarity, when instead we should probably use the word "modern." This proves nothing about atheists, by the way—atheists are not by definition mass murderers. But it does show that Mr. Weinberg's claims about the social consequences of religion and irreligion are at best uninformed and therefore just a bit silly.

His claims about the relationship between science and religion are equally odd, I think. Science through much of the history of the world has been far from antagonistic toward religion; in fact, it has quite often been cared for by and housed in religious institutions. In particular, European science, to which we are heirs today, was given birth and nourished out of Christian and Aristotelian assumptions about creation and order. And increasingly, a growing number of historians of science will tell you that the debate between religion and science that emerged in Europe during the Enlightenment was not a debate between religion and science *per se*, but between two different worldviews, two different ways of thinking about the natural world.

The point is, the enmity Mr. Weinberg assumes between science and religion in many cases is simply not there. Science and religion are not always and necessarily in conflict. It depends upon what religion you're talking about, as well as what science. And that rather simple observation from the history of science is one he fails to appreciate.

Similar problems crop up when he jumps into other fields, such as the social psychology of religion. For example, he asserts that we humans would all be much healthier and happier if only we were liberated from religion altogether. Others have been saying that for years as well. But the problem is, the evidence simply doesn't support it. And I'm not saying this just because brighter folks than he—I'm thinking of Einstein, for example—have come to a different conclusion. I'm saying it because there's quite a bit of evidence that people of religious faith are, on the whole, happier than those without it. They live better. They enjoy life more. They even have better sex lives, for goodness' sake.

So what does all this mean? Simply that when Mr. Weinberg leaves physics and swerves into other disciplines, he's a bad driver. And that again raises the question, "Wouldn't we be better off if God answered Mr. Weinberg's challenge with a flaming sword, despite his contributions to physics? He does so much damage elsewhere, do his contributions in physics really make up for it?" Well, my guess is that plenty of other good scientists would say "Yes! Leave him alone; he's a great physicist," while a few philosophers and historians of religion would say, "It's a close call." All of which means, perhaps Mr. Weinberg's being a good physicist *isn't* reason enough for God to practice forbearance after all.

So let me suggest a second reason why Mr. Weinberg might still be living. Option #2: Because God is God. That's it. Because God is God, and we are not. And there is absolutely nothing in Scripture—from beginning to end—to suggest that God intends to operate on our timetable. Quite the reverse. God does almost nothing according to our calendar, and he tells us nothing—not a thing—about how he has numbered our days. What he gives us in abundance are evidences of his faithfulness to those who love him. That we know for sure. But he rarely tells us what's in store for us just around the corner. And he almost never tells us what he has in store for others.

Nor, for that matter, is God in the business of explaining his every action. Job is a great example. Job, remember, was a righteous man in whom God took great delight. And yet when Job was afflicted with disease and great tragedy and asked God why, what did God say? Basically, "Where were you, Job, when I created the heavens and the earth?" (See Job 38:4-7.) In other words, God never did give Job the answer he wanted, even though Job himself was a good man, who seemed—from our point of view—to deserve an answer.

We may not like this aspect of God, by the way. But it is there whether we like it or not. God is not tame. He does not answer to us; we answer to him. He is not in the dock; the trial is about us. We may not understand why God "causes his sun to rise on the evil [as well as] the good, and sends rain on the righteous, [not just] the unrighteous" (Matthew 5:45). But that's what he does, often as not. And, in like manner, he chose not to send the flaming sword that Mr. Weinberg publicly invited.

And in the absence of his action, some might say, "Score one for Mr. Weinberg." But of course, it was Mr. Weinberg's victory only to the extent that it was also a victory for the chief priests and teachers of the law who mocked Jesus on the cross. Recall that these same priests and teachers had already seen Jesus perform miracle after miracle, including the raising of a man from the dead. They didn't want proof; they wanted a victory. And they thought with Jesus on the cross they were getting it.

But they were wrong. Because God's plans were much grander, much bigger than a simple miracle. The chief priests and scribes wanted Jesus to save himself; God wanted Jesus to save the world. They wanted Jesus to prove himself by coming down from the cross; God wanted Jesus to prove his love by enduring the cross—for our sake, and even for those who were taunting him—to take away the sins of the world.

In other words, in hindsight we know that, at the cross, God was putting his plan of redemption into effect—a plan already in the making at the dawn of creation, a plan that makes the taunts of the chief priests and teachers of the law look like small potatoes. And I suspect that, at some point down the road, that's exactly how we will view the taunts of Nobel laureates today: small potatoes compared to the plans God is putting into effect—not only for us, not only for the world, but for Mr. Weinberg as well.

And with that we come to Option #3, and a final possibility concerning Mr. Weinberg's continuing existence: Perhaps God did not send a flaming sword because of his love for Mr. Weinberg.

You see, here's the problem: If we all got what we deserved when we deserved it, we'd all be goners. History. In that sense, every one of us has been in Mr. Weinberg's shoes. We may not have invited the sword with our lips, but we have all done so with our actions, as well as our inaction. Whenever we do something in the dark that others can't see but that we know is wrong, we invite the sword. Do we honestly think that our gossip about others behind their backs is any less tempting to God than Mr. Weinberg's dare? Do we think that our decisions to ignore the poor, to lust after material wealth, to waste our minds on the junk we feed it are any less offensive, any less deserving of God's judgment than the silly utterances of a very bright man?

Well, you and I know the answer. And what this means, surprisingly, is that God doesn't do what we expect him to do precisely because God is infinitely more gracious and merciful than we would ever be in a million years. God is inscrutable precisely because he is unbelievably longsuffering and infinitely loving.

Unbelievably. That's why *patience* is a fruit of the Spirit, by the way. Because it doesn't come naturally to us. But it does come naturally to God. Which is why we don't always understand him. And why others will not always understand us when we are patient and longsuffering because of the Spirit's work in our lives. When that happens, we will be inscrutable as well. People will say, "Why don't you act to defend yourself? Why turn the other cheek? Give 'em what they deserve! Don't take it any more!" And I suspect that in those moments when we are misunderstood, we may come as close as we can get to understanding our God.

The Graciousness of God

Let me close this chapter with a story. A personal story, which I have been loath to share over the years, because I thought it might be misunderstood. But I think it is time to share it.

During my sophomore year in high school, I suddenly discovered that I had the potential to be a tennis player. Maybe a good one. That had not dawned on me before, because prior to that time I mostly dabbled in tennis, playing just enough to keep up with family and friends. But during my first year in high school, I made the varsity squad and started improving. And by the time I was a sophomore, it was clear that I had a chance, just a chance, of playing varsity singles that year. But it meant that I had to perform well, especially at the beginning of the season.

Things were progressing pretty nicely for me until a rather critical point, at which time I needed to win a very crucial match in order to move up on the roster. And so I did what we Christians often do when we want something badly—I prayed. I followed the formula by trying to make my prayer sound nice. I prayed that everyone would do his best, that everyone would be a good sport, and so on. But the bottom line was, I wanted to win. I was fifteen years old. My friends were watching. "Lord, I don't just want to be good today; I want to be absolutely brutal."

Well, I wasn't. Brutal, that is. I didn't even perform up to my usual level of ability. And the longer the match went on, the more frustrated I got. Not only with myself, but with God as well. With every serve I'd say, "Help me, Lord, help me." And with every serve, I just seemed to get worse and worse. Finally, in desperation I screamed out a cry that would haunt me for days to come—not out loud, mind you, but certainly within earshot of God: "Lord, if you won't help me, then why don't you just get out of my life and leave me alone." I'd had it. Had it with calling and getting no response. Had it with this God who couldn't be counted on. And so I let *him* have it in return.

And do you know what happened? Not a thing, as far as I could tell. My game continued to go miserably. And my God didn't let me go. He didn't help my game, and he didn't let me go. In other words, he was not obedient. Why? Well, at one level it was probably because he had something different in mind for me. Tennis he had in mind for my best friend; for me there were other plans.

But at another level, a deeper level, it was simply because God is gracious and merciful and compassionate beyond reason. And today, can you imagine how grateful I am that God didn't give me the response I deserved? And even asked for? Not only because of eternity. But because of my life today as well. I would be a complete disaster without Christ. A complete and total disaster.

So why doesn't God take our dares and give us what we deserve? For the same reason that Mr. Weinberg is still living. God is merciful and gracious and slow to anger. And if he were not, my friends, we would all be history. Which is the material point. For Mr. Weinberg. And for us as well. Thanks be to God.

4

ON LOVE & TRUTH

(For Pete's Sake)

Most of us have heard a sermon or two on gossip. And we've also no doubt seen those lists of sins in the Bible that one keeps coming across, such as the one from Romans, where gossip is listed alongside a great many other, more interesting sins. And one sort of notices it, and puzzles for a moment, and then goes on with the day.

In other words, we learn—at an early age—that it's not nice to gossip. But at the same time, we see that almost everyone does it, and no one really gets in trouble. I mean, who gets excommunicated for gossiping? In fact, by the time you get to second or third grade, it's pretty hard to imagine life without gossip. It's one of those things you just do—at recess or on the bus or sitting in the cafeteria. In other words, within a few years, for most of us, gossip has already become a major form of entertainment. It happens all the time. For the love of Pete, it hardly seems to matter!

But then one day you become a parent and find yourself caring about someone—your child—in a way you've never quite cared for anyone before in your life. It isn't that you haven't loved before—you love your spouse deeply. That is, hopefully, how you got your child in the first place. But your children . . . they are different. They are, for one thing, vulnerable. Deeply vulnerable. More vulnerable than anyone you've ever loved before.

Babies start off rather a mess, incapable of much of anything besides sucking and crying and doing other things only their parents, and perhaps their grandparents, find tolerable. Human babies have a very limited repertoire, which means that almost everything is up to you, the parent. And nearly your whole life—for a few months at least—becomes devoted just to bringing this little creature into maturity. Holding her, feeding her and whispering all manner of ridiculous things in her ear— it's amazing what even grown men with Ph.D.s will say with a baby in their arms. Amazing. And awesome. And wonderful. Human beings are rarely as totally giving of themselves to another as a parent is in those first few months of a baby's life.

And so you grow attached to your baby. He trusts you in ways you've never been trusted before. She depends on you in ways no one has ever depended on you before. And most parents respond in ways they've never responded before, by completely giving themselves to this little person with no thought of "What's in it for me?" but with great concern for how they can nurture this little being into independence—into becoming a functioning, thriving, whole human being.

Then one day they go off to school and enter the world of "kid-dom." And life is never the same. I remember a particular event that took place when our two older children were still in elementary school. They had been going to a private school since kindergarten—a school we liked a great deal but that was some distance from our home. For quite a few years, we put up with the distance through a creative carpooling arrangement, but eventually that burden become just too much to bear. And so we decided to transfer our children to the local public school, which had quite a good reputation and which we thought would provide a more-than-adequate education.

And we were right in that. What we were wrong about, however—and what we hadn't calculated—was the effect the move would have on our children's lives at the private school between the time of this announcement and their actual transfer. And what was that effect? Not what I imagined, I'll tell you that. I knew it would be hard on my kids because they would be playing on a daily basis with all sorts of friends they knew they were going to have to leave behind. What I didn't realize, however, was how those same "friends" would turn on them once it became known that they were transferring. I mean, it got vicious. And the weapon of choice was . . . the tongue. Friends whom they had known and loved from day one—their closest and best friends—suddenly excluded them, fabricated stories about them and did everything they could to undermine their reputations.

Why? Well, at one level, it's not difficult to figure out. Their friends were probably hurt by their impending departure, probably felt some rejection, and probably thought their decision to attend a public school was an act of disloyalty. That this makes no sense at all, since it wasn't their choice but their parents', is pretty obvious. But it was also irrelevant. For their friends, their transfer was an act of treason, and their friends were going to hold them responsible and make them pay. Which they did through the use of the tongue.

The effect on our kids? Anger at first. Then hurt. And pain. And then, when things really began to sink in, loss of self-confidence, the growing conviction that there must be something wrong with them. Their teachers saw it happen and tried to intervene. But the fact of the matter is that such slander and exclusion made our kids, the victims, feel like their lives were completely ruined. They had lost status. They didn't belong. Their reputations were shot. And our children, who had been growing strong and beautiful, suddenly began to wither right before our eyes.

For parents who have to watch this kind of thing happen, well, it's an unimaginable grief. Unimaginable. These are your children! People you love, whom you've cared for, whom you've nurtured. People who trusted you to make the right decisions for their lives. But it turns out they shouldn't have, because you were the ones who decided to transfer them in the first place, remember? And so you alternate between hating yourself and hating the little beasts you used to think were their friends but who now act like barracuda in a feeding frenzy.

Sticks and Stones

I think what struck me most in that situation was how much easier it would have been if their friends at school had just given them a black eye and then left it at that. You know, have a good tussle and then move on. Physical wounds, after all, usually heal. But when the tongue goes to work, reputations are called into question. Labels are created. And words get etched into the brain so deeply, and so memorably, that the damage is almost incalculable.

And it's always, always permanent. More lives have been shattered, careers thwarted, talents wasted through the choice use of a few words than all the fights and tussles put together. The great lie of the schoolyard playground is that little ditty, "Sticks and stones may break my bones, but names will never

hurt me." Whoever invented that one had the wisdom of a slug.
Bones, you see, can heal. Names, however—words—hang in
the memory like vultures, doing their damage months, even
years, after they're delivered.

So why deliver them? That's the million dollar question. Why
do we do this to one another—not just on the playground as
children, but as adults? In friendships? In churches? In colleges? At work? And more to the point, why do we think it's a
small sin? Or perhaps hardly a sin at all? Nothing in the Bible
suggests that, that's for sure. Paul lists gossip and slander right
up there with murder and debauchery (see Romans 1:24-32).
And James's discussion of the power and destruction of the
tongue is downright bone chilling (see James 3:1-12). It's like a
rudder of a ship, he says—very small, but it sets the course of
the whole ship. It can take you to Honolulu for the time of your
life, or send you right into an iceberg, dashing hopes and
dreams and lives. So why are we so frivolous about words? And
why do we inflict them on one another?

It seems to me that there are several things that prevent us
from taking gossip seriously. The first we've already mentioned—it's so common, and so much a part of the warp and
woof of our lives. And even if we get caught at it, the consequences for us are usually nil. A bit of embarrassment, perhaps.
But nothing we can't dismiss with a momentary, nervous
snicker. It doesn't typically ruin our careers. We don't get sent to
jail for it. It doesn't break up our family. And it appears not to
have all that much of an effect on those about whom we gossip.

I remember when I was a junior in college that there was a
student in one of my classes who I thought was absolutely
obnoxious. He raised his hand almost every time the professor
said anything. He had an opinion—about everything. And he
always thought he was right. Consequently, he would dominate

class sessions with his questions and his very long explanations, and the rest of us would get very irked. Every time his hand went up, we'd roll our heads back and let out audible groans of despair. To no effect, by the way. I mean, the guy was not deterred in the least.

And so what did we do? We gossiped about him. We stabbed him in the back verbally on a regular basis. We'd lay into this guy with a vengeance, reciting his sins (arrogance, conceit, self-centeredness) as well as his personality flaws, which I won't list but which we felt were legion. And of course he became the butt of many jokes, and we had a good time at his expense. To be honest with you, I don't remember ever feeling much guilt about it.

Why is that? Well, for one thing, my classmates and I thought the guy had it coming. He was driving us crazy and using up precious time. We thought he deserved a few choice words. It was even just. But of course, there was more going on than justice— we were also jealous. You see, our classmate happened to be a straight A student. He knew what he was talking about was probably a lot smarter than the rest of us combined. And so instead of taking him on directly outside of class—either to confront his behavior or his ideas—we got personal behind his back. We dismantled his character. We cut him down to size. Our size. And in the process, we made ourselves feel much better.

And we do this all the time, don't we? It's part of the game. It's the way we keep things even and our self-image intact. And generally, "No harm done." In fact, to be honest with you, I doubt my classmates and I actually inflicted all that much damage. I'm not even sure how much he was aware of our banter. Or cared. As you might guess, the guy went right on to graduate school and became a very well-known scholar. No harm done. No effect.

But our gossip did have an effect . . . on us. Or, more precisely, on me. Because, you see, I learned to do with my tongue what James describes in his letter: "With the tongue we praise our Lord and Father, and with it we curse men, who have been made in God's likeness" (James 3:9). James is saying this with thick irony, by the way. He's saying, how can you do this? How can you praise God on the one hand, and then demean those whom God has made in his likeness on the other? The answer is that you can't. Which means that your praise of God is devoid of meaning. It's hypocrisy. If you knew the One you were praising, and you really believed human beings reflected his image, you would not—*could* not—slander them.

So the first thing we need to keep in mind when we talk about a person behind his or her back is that it reveals something rather disturbing, not about that person but about ourselves. It reveals, fundamentally, a lack of understanding of and genuine love for God. And as we spew forth our diatribes, we ought to know that we are, at that moment, giving public display to the size of our heart.

But we are revealing something else as well. We are showing others that we are not trustworthy. Make no mistake, your friends and co-workers are not dumb. They know good and well that if you are willing to talk about others behind their backs, you will be willing to do the same to them. They will trust you less. And all your relationships will be affected. They will not go deep. They will not be marked by candor. And you will not be able to rely on them, especially when the chips are down. In this way, your sin will come back to haunt you, as it always does. For precisely what you had hoped to gain by demeaning others—a little ego satisfaction and social regard—is exactly what you will lose in the long run. The reputation you demean through slander and gossip is primarily your own.

I'm getting a little worked up about this, aren't I? And you
want to know why? Because I'm a scholar by training and a
teacher at heart. And I have come to believe that slander and
gossip—sins of the tongue, if you will—are especially easy, and
especially deadly, in communities where learning is seen as
central. Like churches, for example. Or schools, at all levels. We
deal in words, we teachers and preachers. That is our stock in
trade. Speaking, reading, writing. The expression of ideas.
Words are what we are about. And those who teach and study
"do words" pretty well. That's why we're here. That's why we've
been chosen. Precisely for that reason, however, words not only
provide the greatest opportunity, but also the greatest danger—
for faculty, students and preachers alike. Through words, people can flourish, grow deep in the truth, get glimpses of the Creator. But through them, too, people can be crushed, hurt, led
astray. And when that happens, it not only brings pain on those
who are their target, but it fundamentally undermines the mis-
sion and reason for being of an institution devoted to the pursuit of truth.

Let me say it boldly: Whenever we slander another person or
gossip about someone behind his or her back, we bring evidence against ourselves. We say for all the world to see, "I do
not care about the truth. You can't trust my words. I do not love
God nearly as much as I love myself."

And when that happens, everything you value goes down the
drain. You may still get straight A's. Your church may grow by
leaps and bounds. You may go on to publish books, land great
jobs and win great honors. You may still affirm God's Word as
true. But you will have lost a heart for truth, for growing deep in
wisdom and understanding, for learning to love God and
neighbor, for bringing light to a world in darkness. And every
time you snicker at a classmate behind their back, or pass along

juicy tidbits about a parishioner, or cut down a fellow teacher or pastor, you say to the world, "I am a fraud, as is this place where I teach or preach or study." And both you and your sanctuary lose their reason for being.

Strong words? I did not invent them. James begins the third chapter of his letter with this warning, "Not many of you should presume to be teachers, . . . because you know that we who teach will be judged more strictly." In today's context, I believe that admonition applies to every Christian who is teaching at a church or school, the select few who have been chosen to be educated in depth to serve a needy world. Our words, our judgments about others, will testify either for or against us. As we have judged, so shall we be judged—to our glory, or to our dismay.

Truth Matters

I began with a story about my children and their encounter with gossip at a private school early in their lives. What I didn't tell you, however, is that they eventually transferred to the other school, kicked the dust off their feet, and through the grace of God and a lot of hard work blossomed into two of the finest human beings I know. I am prejudiced, of course. But I am also amazed. And grateful beyond words.

But there was another person in the story: me, their father, who had to sit back and watch this thing go on for months and bear the burden of a parent whose children were being verbally annihilated right before his eyes and not be able to do anything about it. And then suddenly, in the middle of the pain I was feeling for my children, almost as if on cue, I began to remember.

I remember, first, a time when I was in junior high, and one of the kids in my Sunday school class—from a rival town—

became the butt of my jokes. And I thought it was great fun to tell stories at his expense until one day, at a church gathering, his father came up to me and said, "Stan, what do you have against my son?" I was surprised at the time. But I was never able to shake off the tone of his voice or the pain in his eyes, even without understanding. And now, as a parent myself, I not only recalled his pain, I understood it. To my shame and my horror.

Another time soon came to mind, when I passed along a piece of information, in confidence, to a friend. The information was about someone I had known in high school who had grown up to gain quite a good reputation as a writer and speaker. Like most people of accomplishment, her high school *persona* did not quite match her eventual stature. In fact, in high school she was a bit of a "floozy," as we used to say—a woman of the world, who seemed much more interested in members of the opposite sex than in studies. And this seemed to me to be an interesting fact, so I chose to pass it along to my friend. No harm done, I thought; we laughed, and I told him to keep it confidential.

But he didn't. In fact, he passed it on—directly to the former "floozy" herself. And suddenly, not only did *she* know her reputation was being tarnished and that I couldn't be trusted; but *I* knew that my friend, with whom I had shared the information in confidence, could not be trusted either. One little piece of information, and it wound up undermining not only the victim's reputation and my own, but also the reputation of my friend. I never trusted him again. With anything. Never again shared anything deep or worthy or personal. Because I could not trust him. Nor could he trust me.

Still in the midst of parental angst, I continued remembering—this time recalling an event that happened when I was in graduate school. I was listening to a conversation between one of my favorite professors and a fellow graduate student while I sat outside the professor's office waiting for my turn to come in. And they were talking loudly, with great gusto. About the great ideas of the Western world? No. They were discussing the great stupidity of Pete, one of my classmates. Pete, who happened to say things my professor didn't appreciate. Pete, whose political stance my professor found offensive. And so he roasted him. Doubted his intelligence. Doubted his ancestry. Questioned just about everything else he could about him and had a very good time doing it.

To my knowledge, it had no impact upon my professor's behavior toward Pete. He always treated him respectfully in class. And I believe Pete wound up getting an A. So, "No harm done," I'm sure the professor thought. Just a little venting, a little fun with words, at no one's real expense.

But I heard. And so did the graduate student who was in his office that day, with whom he shared the amusement. And the effect on me was substantial. I never quite trusted that professor again, not just with political opinions, but with any observation. In his class, I kept my mouth shut. And in my heart, I didn't trust his conclusions about the course's content either. If he couldn't separate his ego from the truth while talking with a student in his office, what made me think he could do it in class? Or in what he wrote, for that matter? The truth was obviously much less important to him than he was to himself. It was the last class I took from him, and his impact on my thinking was, from that day on, nil.

Gossip matters. Because truth matters. Gossip is one of the small sins, we say, because we do it all the time. But every time we do it, we not only hurt someone else's reputation, but we testify to our own. Why? Because there is always someone sitting out in the hall. Someone who is listening in. Always a parent. Always a friend. Always someone who looks up to you—who hears, who knows and who cares. And always, always a heavenly Father—who hears, who knows and who cares. Our assumptions about privacy when we gossip are the assumptions of a fool. And our credibility as individuals, as well as the credibility of the learning community of which we are a part, is always on the line.

> Who is wise and understanding among you? Let him show it by his good life, by deeds done in the humility that comes from wisdom. But if you harbor bitter envy and selfish ambition in your hearts, do not boast about it or deny the truth. . . . For where you have envy and selfish ambition, there you find disorder and every evil practice.

> But the wisdom that comes from heaven is first of all pure; then peace-loving, considerate, submissive, full of mercy and good fruit, impartial and sincere. Peacemakers who sow in peace raise a harvest of righteousness." (James 3:13-18)

Love is displayed in word *and* deed because it is rooted in the heart—a heart that loves the truth.

5

ON Love & feeLING

(So, What About Sex?)

It is a curious thing. In my many years of initiating obnoxious conversations, I have never been told that sex is a sure route to happiness. That is, if you ask a friend in a reflective moment what makes them happy, "sex" is a highly improbable answer. They might say something about people they enjoy being with. Or moments they have savored. But they will not say, "Sex." Not if they're serious, at least. It's an answer that doesn't match the question.

And yet, if you watch the way we live, that's exactly what you might conclude. If you look at how we spend our money or how we dress or the forms of entertainment we pursue, sex is clearly at the center of much that we do.

So what's going on? What is the relationship between sex and happiness? Why is sex so central in our behavior but so marginal to our articulated beliefs?

Sex is different. You learn that early on. For one thing, you don't talk about it at the dinner table. No one says, "You know, I

was having sex today when the funniest thing happened . . ."
You just don't do that—except, of course, for Jerry Springer, or
some other yahoo who takes pleasure in emotional strip tease.
But the rest of the time, when we're in the real world, talking
with real people, sex is not a matter of routine conversation.
And, on the whole, I think most of us are kind of glad that's the
case.

Nevertheless, that's a problem. Because we think about sex—
a lot. Especially when we're young—when the hormones are on
the move and we're not. Especially in this culture where sexuality is so readily flaunted and so often idolized. Though we don't
talk about sex, we dress and act to signal sexuality. Though we
don't discuss sex at the dinner table, we watch television and
movies and advertisements that are simply dripping with sexual
messages, most of which are aimed at getting us to buy something or do something, and all of which are intent upon engaging us emotionally. And so we *are* engaged. On a daily basis.

So what happens? Well, a lot of things. Early on, for example,
we are likely to conclude that sex must be incredibly wonderful
(that's why we think about it all the time) and incredibly evil
(that's why we don't talk about it very much). That's especially
probable in Christian homes, where sex is likely to be discussed
less than usual, but where people are nevertheless fully satu-
rated with the values of the culture. I don't mean, by the way,
that this is how we verbalize it. Few of us would admit to such a
double standard. But deep in our consciousness, it is there nevertheless. On the one hand, we think that a good round of sex
with the partner of choice is likely to be the best thing available
this side of heaven. On the other hand, what a despicable thing
that would be. What a *deliciously* despicable thing that would be!

When we check a reliable source on truth and wisdom, however (I'm suggesting the Bible here), what we discover is that

neither conclusion is justified. In the first place, there is nothing evil about sex whatsoever. The creation story, in both Genesis 1 and 2, makes it clear that God created us as sexual beings and that this was part of his good plan. We were to be fruitful and multiply. And we were to be naked and not ashamed. In other words, we were created to have sex and to enjoy its consequences. And God said this is good.

The problem, of course, comes after the Fall, after sin invades our domain. But that doesn't change the basic nature of sex. Sex is still good. What the Fall changes is the way we think about and use sex, which gets us to the second point: Sex ain't all that good. Of course, when I use the term "good" here, I don't mean it in the qualitative sense that God meant it in describing his creation. Sex is a qualitatively good thing. But it is not the end all, the final frontier, the surest route to happiness as our culture often leads us to believe it is. It is not, to put it more precisely, a true end that human beings were designed to pursue.

And we know that, right? At some level, we know the cultural version of sex is a myth. That's why no one says, "Sex" when asked about happiness. But the truth is, at a deeper level, we believe the culture more than our convictions. Our knowledge about sex and our feelings are on a collision course. Sex is important to us. Very. And the question is, Why? Why this fascination, this fixation, with sex?

At first blush, that's a dumb question, isn't it? Sex is fun. We all know that. It's pleasurable. Enjoyable. True enough. But so is sliding into a hot tub of water at the end of the day. Or savoring a warm lobster, dripping with melted butter. Those are pretty good as well, are they not? You enjoy them. You're happy to have them. You even look forward to them, now and then. But do you think about them constantly? Do you make them the center of your life so that they determine how you dress, what you say, how you act? Or, to be a bit more brutal, would you jump into a hot tub if you thought you might get pregnant? Would you eat a lobster if you thought you might contract AIDS? Of course not. You wouldn't even consider it. And, similarly, very few of us would allow our lives to revolve around hot baths or lobster or just about any of the other good pleasures that God, in his graciousness, has given us.

But we do when the pleasure is sex. Why is that? Why this special fascination with sex? I want to suggest that it has absolutely nothing to do with the physical pleasure of sex and everything—everything—to do with its meaning. Sex means more to us than a hot bath. And it's supposed to.

The Meaning of Sex
Sex is supposed to mean that you and another have become one. A union. A holy partnership. It means that you have given yourselves to one another completely, without reservation. It is that moment when we can legitimately pretend to be back in the Garden, before the Fall, Adam and Eve, enjoying one another's nakedness and not being ashamed.

And precisely because sex, in its meaningfulness, gets us so close to the Garden, its meaningful *distortion* is such a prize— and such a necessity for the Evil One. Because if he wins here, if he can distort the meaning of sex for us, then he has ruined one of our best opportunities to know and rejoice in the intentions of the Creator.

So I think it is not surprising that we are pretty stupid where sex is concerned and that we have come to believe a whole cluster of lies about sex in this culture. And the first is that sex is a physical act without any ultimate meaning. We know this is a lie by virtue of the way we act. No one behaves as if sex were just like eating a good lobster. And yet people justify the abuse of sex in precisely those terms, calling it a "craving," an "urge" or a "need" that must be satisfied, and then laughing it off as having "sown their wild oats."

We follow up the lie that sex lacks any ultimate meaning with a second contradictory but equally fallacious assumption: that the joy of sex is dependent upon competition; that the only good sex is that which comes at the end of a game of cat and mouse. We assume that the harder the chase, and the more attractive the objective, the more enjoyable the catch. But instead, all we get are unfulfilled cats. And emotionally dead mice.

Finally, we come to the most tempting lie of all: the idea that sex should be an expression of the love two people feel for each other and that it is therefore appropriate wherever, and whenever, true love exists. This is the standard typically used in our culture—it accounts for most of the "good sex" we see on television or in the theater—and, generally, most of us buy into it. Indeed, it is such a relief, and such a departure from the various kinds of debauched sex we have to put up with, that it is almost a comfort when it occurs. How many times have you found yourself sitting in a movie theater rooting for love and sex to be conjoined, rather than held apart, only to discover in the end that you have just been rooting for adultery. How can that be?

Well, it *can* be because sex linked to love substantially buys into a biblical view of sexuality. To say that sex ought to be an expression of love is to admit that sex is special, something set apart, even holy. And that's certainly right. We even refer to the act of sex as "making love." To say that sex is special, moreover, is to admit that sex has meaning and that its meaning needs to be paid attention to. So you can't just have sex whenever and with whomever you wish. Finally, connecting the meaning of sex with the notion of *love* captures a rather important concept in a biblical worldview. To say that sex ought to be an expression of feeling love for another person, therefore, is to move substantially in the right direction.

But once we start down that path we seem to get ourselves into all kinds of trouble. For example, people sometimes use that idea to justify dissolving a marriage—even an admittedly good one—in order to begin a relationship with someone new. Imagine that you're married but you no longer feel passionately in love with your spouse. Instead, you're head over heels in love with someone else. Since sex legitimately flows from feelings of love, how could you not express yourself sexually in this new relationship? And though you may still care for your spouse, how could you carry on a fulfilling sexual relationship with that person after the flames of passion have died out? True love demands that you divorce—it's the only "honest" thing to do.

The same idea—that sex ought to be an expression of love—constitutes the justification for any number of sexual relationships before marriage as well, doesn't it? Think of how sex is portrayed in even the best movies or on the best TV programs these days. Or, to go from fiction to fact, think about your own friends and acquaintances who are sexually active. Don't most of them justify their activity on the basis of love? And didn't they do so with their previous partner? And the one before that?

The point is, the idea that sex should be an expression of love may give sex all kinds of internal meaning—and may make us feel very good about the various kinds of sexual relationships we get into—but from the outside it doesn't seem much different from sex practiced for any other reason. It still justifies sex on demand. It still legitimizes sex outside of marriage. And it still doesn't look anything like the concept God had in mind when he created us in the first place. In other words, though it *seems* beautiful and meaningful, it still doesn't get us back to the Garden. Indeed, it leaves us stuck in a world where sex becomes a vehicle for tearing families and relationships apart, for practicing serial monogamy, all in the name of love. Something is wrong. What is it?

Well, I know what you're thinking. You're thinking the problem here is that, while the connection between love and sex is a good one, not all love should be expressed sexually. Right? Thus the reason some folks get into difficulty is that they make the wrong choices about when love should, or shouldn't, result in sex.

I don't think so. I don't think the problem with the love-and-sex thesis is simply a matter of timing. The problem, I believe, is the thesis itself. Indeed, I want to suggest—as blasphemous as it might seem—that the pairing of love and sex is quite wrong, at least wrong given the way our culture defines these terms. The problem here is our understanding of the term "love." As we tend to use the concept, love for us is a feeling, an emotion. For that reason, we talk about "falling in love," as though we had no choice in the matter. We are smitten. Our hearts are touched. And suddenly, we're in love.

Now there is nothing wrong with the feeling of love. In fact, I'm all in favor of warm hearts. Have one myself. But to make the feeling of love the basis for sex is dangerous, because feelings are flighty. They change. They can justify sex with any number of people, places or things. And, indeed, they do.

The purpose of sex, I would contend, is not *your* feelings but the feelings of someone else. It exists not to make *you* feel a certain way, but to make *someone else* feel a certain way. Sex itself is not a feeling, it's a gift. It's a gift of love from you to someone else. It is not aimed at receiving something, but giving something. For that reason, sex at its best is not driven by feelings of smittenness or stomach butterflies or thumping hearts—all of which have to do with *you*, how someone makes *you* feel, and which (nine times out of ten) are based upon how popular that certain someone is. It is not driven by what a great catch you've made, or how, in any number of ways, it makes you feel rather proud of yourself for having landed such a hunk, such a babe, such a bod.

Now don't get me wrong. I am not saying that these feelings are illegitimate; they may or may not be. To be honest, it doesn't much matter, because you're going to have them anyway. What's wrong here is not the feeling, but the connection between the feeling of love and sex, and the idea that such feelings ought to be the justification for, and eventually result in, a sexual relationship. Why do I say that? Well, look around. We live in a culture that has made the connection between sex and feeling in love paramount. So, how is it going? Are people feeling good about their sexuality? Are relationships stronger than ever? Is the family doing well? Is marriage a source of happiness and fulfillment for most people?

Let's bring it a little closer to home: How is this assumption about sex and feelings working among your friends and acquaintances? Is courtship going well? Are males and females relating to each other as human beings created in the image of God? Do lovers have respect for one another? Do they treat each other with mutual care, gentleness and kindness? Do dating relationships build each partner up, not destroy? Are values being upheld? Is righteousness being maintained?

And, to bring it all the way home, how are you feeling about your sexuality—past, present and future? Is the assumption that sex and feelings go together working out well for you? How's it working out for the object of your affections, if you're married? Is that person content with his or her sexuality? Are you? Will you be content if you get married? If you don't?

Another question: How does the Bible define love? Is it viewed primarily as a feeling you have? Or is it something you do, something you give? Listen to the apostle Paul as he describes love in his first letter to the Corinthians: "Love is patient, love is kind. It does not envy, it does not boast, it is not proud. It is not rude, it is not self-seeking, it is not easily angered, it keeps no record of wrongs. Love does not delight in evil but rejoices with the truth. It always protects, always trusts, always hopes, always perseveres. Love never fails" (1 Corinthians 13:4-8).

What strikes me about this list is that almost every one of the things Paul says love is *not* relates to a feeling about the self. Love does not "envy" or "boast"; it is not "proud," "rude" or "self-seeking." Notice the focus: envy and pride are feelings you have about yourself based on how you stack up against others, and they result in self-centered behavior.

Now listen again to what love *is*: It is "patient" and "kind." It "protects," "trusts," "hopes" and "perseveres." Those are all qualities that relate *not* to how we feel about ourselves but to how we treat others. We are patient and kind to others; we protect and trust others. Love moves us away from navel gazing, away from self-absorption, away from being consumed with our own feelings.

And so, what we discover—surprise of surprises—is that the union of sex and love in a biblical framework means almost exactly the opposite of what our culture says it means. Sex rooted in love, as the Bible defines love, doesn't have much to do with how you feel, but it has everything—everything—to do with the physical and emotional well being of the one you love.

For this reason, feeling-based sex—which our culture advocates—routinely generates every one of the negative characteristics mentioned by Paul: envy, pride, rudeness, boasting, self-seeking. That almost sounds like a compendium of modern sexuality. And it's exactly what Paul says love is *not*.

Love-based sex, on the other hand, is *patient*—it can wait until it's right, no problem. It is *kind*—it would never push someone beyond his or her standards, much less one's own. It *protects*—protects the other's reputation, honor, safety. It wouldn't harm a flea. Love-based sex *trusts*—since it isn't based on competition, it doesn't worry about what has happened in the past, nor does it assume the worst for the present. Why? Because it *keeps no record of wrongs*. Love-based sex *hopes*—it hopes for the best for the other person, even if, heaven forbid, the best might mean "not me." Love-based sex *perseveres*—it is not a one-night stand, or even a long-term relationship. Love-based sex perseveres forever. Because love *never fails*.

Finally, love-based sex *rejoices in the truth*. It seems sort of odd to be talking about sex and truth in the same breath, doesn't it? What's truth got to do with it? Well, biblical love has everything in the world to do with truth. It rejoices in the truth because it is rooted in the truth. And what is the truth that provides the foundation for love-based sex? Simply this: When God created the heavens and the earth, he made humans, like all other animals, sexual beings. And he said, that's good.

But for us—for those he created in his own image—he gave sex a special meaning. That's why your cocker spaniel only has sex when she's in heat, and you think about it all the time. Unlike to your spaniel, sex is meaningful to you. And what is the meaning and purpose your Creator intended? That sex should be an expression of God's love between a man and a woman, who leave their parents and become one flesh. For that reason, it is patient and kind. It protects, trusts, hopes and perseveres. And, of course, it never fails, it never ends.

When appreciated and practiced in that way, sex brings life, just as our Creator intended. When it isn't, it brings death. In either case, it won't make you happy. That wasn't its purpose. But it can be the occasion for you to express your love to another, completely and without reservation. With great joy and meaningful delight. And, curiously enough, to your utter astonishment, that will make you happy. And that's the truth in which love-based sex rejoices.

6

on Love & grace

(Going to Hell)

Okay, here's the situation. A friend of ours and her grandson were together one day, doing grandparenty-type things, which is another way of saying that the little guy was in the process of being spoiled rotten. All of a sudden, right out of the blue, the grandson—who's around nine—comes up with this question: "Nauna," he says, "Don't you think hell is just a little bit harsh?"

Children are smart. But not as smart as grandmothers. Which is why Nauna, in this case, had the good sense to answer the question with a smile, a pat on the head and another candy bar. Her husband, who is not so smart, wasn't there at the time. Which is good. Because his response, when he heard the question (Isn't hell a bit harsh?) was, "I think that's the point." Proving again what we all know, that grandfathers aren't quite as bright as grandmothers.

Just kidding. But it struck me—being male, and a potential grandfather, and therefore not so smart—that this really is a

good question. A great question, in fact. And you know that
because of how people react to the story. They don't yawn, for
example, or assume it's silly or irrelevant. Nor do they hush it up
or consider it a great offense ("Don't say that, or even think
that."). Instead, there is almost always a smile. And usually a
laugh. And the realization that the little fellow has expressed
something, rather artfully, that all of us have thought before at
one time or another.

And that makes it a great question. Especially for those of us
who describe ourselves as evangelicals, in this culture, in these
days. Here's the deal. We evangelicals want to be biblical people, people of the Book. We want that, not to be different from
other Christians, but to be the same: to be a part of the same
faithful tradition that has carried the gospel forward, from the
time of Christ to the present age. And so we are not fundamentally people of any particular denomination (since over the last
2,000 years, that faithful remnant has been a part of many different churches and denominations), we are people of Christ,
who want to follow him, faithfully and fully, regardless of the
age in which we live.

And that's the problem, it seems to me. Because the age we're
in, and the culture, find the concept of hell to be just a little odd.
Unnerving. Unfair, in fact. Not particularly forgiving. Not toler-
ant. Harsh, to use a modern idiom. I mean, why would a good
God, who is fair and just and gracious and merciful and above
all loving, come up with something like hell in the first place?
But more importantly, send people there, which is the material
point. Isn't that, indeed, just a bit harsh?

So that's problem number one. But here's problem number
two, for those who want to be faithful followers of Christ: it is
precisely Jesus, in all of the Bible, who speaks the most forcefully and fully about hell. In fact, we don't have a lot about hell

in the Bible outside of the teachings of Jesus. Not from Paul, whose teachings usually get us in the soup in this culture. And not from many of the Old Testament writers, who were not afraid of being brutally frank. It is from Jesus, and also John in his Revelation—John, whom Jesus loved, and who makes love absolutely central in his letters—that we get all this business about hell. And it makes you wonder: Why?

At least it does me. And that's problem number three. Because I'm not a theologian. Nor a biblical scholar. Nor particularly bright, as we've already seen. I mean, chances are, I'm going to be a grandfather some day. So I've got three strikes against me. But I do like good questions. And I think in this culture, in these days, this is a good question. Why does this Truth, this "gentle Jesus, meek and mild," talk so much about hell? And what does it have to do with the way we live our lives, as his followers, in our quest for happiness? Well, let me throw out a few possibilities. Four possibilities, in fact. Four reasons why, upon reflection, hell makes a lot of sense to me.

Why Hell?

Reason #1: Justice. You and I, because of the culture we are in, and also because of what has happened to theology over the years, are not inclined to think a lot about justice, especially in relation to God. We think of God as love, which is good, and we think of justice as something very different from love. Which is not so good.

For example, what would you say is the most basic characteristic of God? At his core, God is . . . what? Love, right? And I think that is right. And yet, biblical scholars through the ages, when thinking about the most basic characteristic of God, have sometimes chosen justice over love. Jewish scholars have been especially inclined that way, and frankly without the Gospels, I can see why. God from the beginning shows himself to be deeply and passionately concerned with justice—right living. And in fact, the need for an atoning lamb—the need for Christ's sacrifice, on the cross, on our behalf—is precisely because of God's justice. God does not willy-nilly excuse our shameful living. Our sins matter. They matter so much that our forgiveness cost Jesus his life.

So God cares about justice, in the Old Testament as well as the New. And for that reason, hell makes sense to me. Let's face it, if there was no hell, justice would be in trouble. Why? Well, for one thing, there are things done, deeds committed, which absolutely cry out for hell. Adolf Hitler and Pol Pot—two men who shed the blood of millions of innocent people: Do you honestly think that justice was served when these two men died? I mean, Hitler took his own life. And Pol Pot lived many years after the killing fields, assuming he's not living now. And frankly, regardless of how they died, their mere deaths are simply not enough to satisfy any concept of justice that I'm aware of. Not enough. Not enough!

We can forget that, being somewhat distant from Auschwitz or Cambodia. But you will not forget it if you sit down and talk with someone who went through it; whose parent or brother or friend went through it. They may, by God's grace, be able to forgive. But they will never forget the pain, the tragedy, the loss that they endured. And, of course, to get the full picture, you have to multiply what they endured by millions to fully appreciate the injustice.

And those are just two notorious examples. The fact is, people do horrendous things for their own pleasure, and get away with them. Live long lives. Die in luxury and fine linens, in their sleep. And if that is all they get for their deeds—mere death, well . . . it ain't good enough. And I suspect that if it's not good enough for me, miserable fool that I am, it's not going to be good enough for a God who cares deeply and passionately about justice and who is a friend of the innocent, the poor, the orphan, the victim. A God who cares for even the sparrow will not let Hitler finish his flight in death.

So, Reason #1: Justice requires hell; at least in some cases, and for some people, there needs to be a hell to keep our understanding of a just God intact. Which leads to Reason #2: We need hell to remind us of the consequences of our own sin. You see, right now, we're all thinking, "Yep, Hitler was bad; he deserves hell; and I'm sure glad that I'm not a Hitler 'cause he's in trouble." And that's true. But are we not in trouble as well? Is there really such a vast difference between Adolf Hitler and Stan Gaede? Is there? Really?

Well, at one level, there certainly is. I—we—haven't engaged in genocide. We haven't killed millions, at least not in the literal sense. But how many have we killed with our words? With our false tales? With our calculated ignorance? That last one, especially, gives me pause. How easy it is for us to turn a blind eye toward those things we are doing, and not doing, which reap a whirlwind for others. We throw away food while others starve and think almost nothing of it. Does God? We crucify a co-worker with our words when he or she's not around and consider it a mere joke. Does God? We use our power to promote ourselves at others' expense and excuse it by saying, "That's just the way the world is; that's what you have to do to succeed." Does God?

And why do we do these things? Well, we're sinners, that's why. From day one. But we also think of sin poorly, it seems to me. Which is how the deceiver works. What images come to mind when you think of sin? I mean, right now, what are you thinking when I say *sin*? Or what were you thinking before I

gave examples of gossip or materialism? Well, it probably
depends upon your age. If you're young, it probably had something to do with sex. If you're in your thirties, on the other
hand, it still probably had to do with sex! Or tax fraud. Or some
other obvious abuse. Which is good. We should probably be
even more sensitive than we are to such things. But what we
should not do is miss the fact that sin is much bigger than sex.
And much more destructive.

In fact, sex isn't the problem at all; it's a gift. Nor is food the
problem; it's a gift. Nor are words a problem; they are a gift. The
problem is when we use these good gifts, which God has given
us, to destroy, not build up. Sin, remember, is fundamentally
about deception. Deception which leads us to reject the good
and seek after those things that lead to death instead. Our
death. And the death of others. When we lust after our neighbor's spouse instead of loving our own, we begin to kill: our
neighbor, our spouse, and ourselves. When we lust after food
instead of gratefully and responsibly enjoying our portion, we
begin to kill: our neighbor who is starving, our own bodies
which are not. When we lust after fame, we begin to kill: our
neighbor with our words of assassination, ourselves with our
conceit, our pride, our arrogance.

And I could go on and on. But there is no need. Because you
and I know in our hearts that what I'm saying is true. Our sin is
bad stuff. It destroys lives. Brings death. Has consequences. And
deserves judgment. And Jesus says that's exactly what will happen. And we would be well served, I think, to keep that in mind.

Reason #3: I think we need hell to remind us of what we
have—and what we don't have—in God. I am reminded here of
a statement that has become very popular in the last few years
when discussing hell. The statement is typically offered up as a
way of understanding hell, and it is something to the effect that

hell is essentially separation from God. In fact, my guess is that this statement has become the current way of defining hell among evangelicals. What is hell? It's separation from God.

And that seems right to me. Except for the fact that it usually comes in the context of trying to explain hell to someone who is asking our question of the morning. Isn't hell just a bit harsh? "Yes, well, . . . but try to think of hell as separation from God; you reject God, and you're eventually separated from him; and that's hell." The implication is that this definition makes hell sound both more reasonable and a little less horrifying. And what bothers me in this whole exchange isn't the definition of hell but the assumption that separation from God is less horrifying than a lake of fire or any of the other biblical depictions of hell. That seems to me to misunderstand the use of metaphor, for one thing, and the implications of separation, for another.

Look, why does the Bible describe hell as a lake of fire, utter darkness, a place of tears, et cetera? It is clearly not an attempt to describe precisely the nature of hell because some of the images contradict one another; you have light and darkness at the same time, for example. These are pictures—metaphors— which are there to tell us something. And the clear message is that hell is *worse* than anything one can imagine or describe, not better.

Let's take an opposite image. How would you describe love to someone who didn't quite get the concept? How would you do it? You wouldn't describe it precisely because there is no such description. You would describe it metaphorically, which is what we always do. Love is like a flower that blooms in the morning and grows in beauty and has a wonderful aroma. Not. Well, let's see. Love is like a sunset in Santa Barbara, with the sun just breaking over the horizon in the west, and a full moon rising over the mountains in the southeast. That's a little better because the moon in Santa Barbara is about as good as it gets. Especially a full moon in the summer, early in the evening, rising over the mountains in the southeast, and then moving over the ocean, and casting a path of moonlight from the islands right into the bay. My, oh my, it's just fabulous! And it's a little bit like love. Just a little bit. In his letter, John perhaps says it best, when he says, this is love, that you lay down your life for another.

You see you can't describe love adequately with a definition. All you can do is give examples, metaphors, analogies that get at the concept. And the point is not that love is equal to any of those examples, and certainly not less, but more—more wonderful, more beautiful, more grand. And that's what I think is going on with these images of hell, except in reverse. Hell is separation from God. But that's not less horrendous than all these images of hell, it's more. The images are there to tell us something. And the something is: Being separated from God is awful. More awful than anyone can imagine.

That fact, and our tendency not to "get it," says a lot about our concept of God, by the way. We really don't think of God as good, do we? We think of him as the source of goodies, perhaps, which he dispenses periodically, in his whim, or when we've been good. But we don't appreciate him fully as good and beautiful and wonderful, better than anything we could imagine or dream of, including full moons over Santa Barbara. We don't. We take most of his goodness for granted. I think that's part of the deception, by the way, one of the deceiver's great victories in our lives.

That we don't regularly wake up feeling stunned by the morning in all its beauty and majesty and wonder is an abomination, I think. That we don't lie down at night seeing the foggy dew on the trees or hearing the sounds of night critters or seeing the stars as thick as sugar against a jet black sky—that we don't see and hear all of that and weep for joy—is just amazing. That we don't regularly marvel at how our bodies work, what our eyes take in, the music our ears hear, the various tastes our tongues can hardly describe they're so varied, the things we can learn and enjoy—that we can do all these things, every day, and not drop down on our knees in worship and wonder—well, that is the wonder. That is the wonder!

Let's face it, we are immensely myopic to all the goodness and beauty that surrounds us. And for that reason we forget what we have in God. What we have, and what would be lost if we lost him. If we were separated from him, it would be hell, my friends. It *would* be hell. And that's the point.

But that's not the last point, nor the end of the story. Which takes us Reason #4: We are not left in hell. The story of Jesus does not end with condemnation, but redemption. It ends with Jesus giving up his life on the cross—for our sake, taking on our sin, dying in our stead, redeeming us from the pit—and rising again to new life with us. You want to know why we need hell? So we might understand what we have in Christ.

Let me tell you the real tragedy of hell, or how we Christians think about hell. I would guess that a majority of the conversations I've been in concerning hell have been about one question. And it is the question of who is going there. And almost always, it's about people we don't know, people in particular circumstances, often contrived, whose future seems in doubt. What about the fellow raised on a remote island, who never had the chance to hear about Christ? What about the girl who died at the age of four, who may or may not have reached the age of accountability? What about people who have heard about Jesus, but their hearing was impaired by their psychological state, their social condition or the heretical form in which the message was delivered: what will happen to them? And the questions go on and on. As do we.

You want to know what my greatest fear was penning this chapter on hell? It was that a reader would leave this chapter with those kinds of questions in mind and miss the point. Don't do that. Please, don't do that. Because the point is not about someone else, in a hypothetical situation, or even someone else you know. It's about you. It's about me. I love the way Aslan deals with these questions in the Chronicles of Narnia. Do you remember? In almost every book, someone wonders about the fate of another person. And what is Aslan's response? "That's not your story," says Aslan. That's not your story.

When we come to the end of our journey, my friends, and meet our Maker, the question will not be about Jim or John or Mary. It will be about us. It will be about me. And, for that reason, that had better be the question we wrestle with today.

The Bottom Line
So let me tell you what I know about me. And about hell. What I know for sure is that I am a sinner—that I have, from my earliest memory, asserted the rule of my self over the kingdom of God. That I have repeatedly put myself first, my neighbor second and God someplace way down the line. Sometimes I do all of this intentionally; other times almost against my will. But it's there. And I know it's wrong. And I do it anyway.

And there is not a doubt in my mind that I deserve the path I have chosen. In fact, why wouldn't a righteous God simply let me walk right off the cliff, if that's what I want to do? That's the question I can't answer, by the way. That's the real puzzler for me. If I repeatedly seek my own way, if I continually pursue my own course and build my own kingdom, why would he even give me a second thought? Why not just wave goodbye and let me reap the consequences of my own corruption?

That's what we would do, is it not? That's what we do all the time, in fact, with our own so-called friends. When they reject us. Despitefully use us. Do we continue to care for them, provide for them, shower them with beauty and music and everything else that makes life possible (assuming we could)? Well, of course not. Minimally, we turn on our heels and walk the other way. More likely, we flatten them (assuming we could).

But God did not. God, in his infinite grace and mercy, decided—in a way that I cannot comprehend—to love me in spite of who I am and what I deserve. And to rescue me from the hell I seem forever bent on choosing. Sending to me, instead, Jesus. My Jesus. Who lived the life I should have lived. Who died the death I should have died. Who paid the price for the sins I committed. And then said to Stan Gaede—this twerp from nowhere—follow me. Follow me! Not to hell, but to life. The life I wanted you to have from the beginning.

That's the amazing part, to me. About hell. And about our good and gracious God who, for whatever reason, seems bent on breaking almost all the rules to keep me from going there. I don't know why he did it. But I, for one, am not going to forget it. Not going to forget to praise him daily, with my lips and my life, for what he has accomplished for me. It's just too grand. Too great. It's just too amazing.

What makes me happy, deep in my bones, in the darkest moments of the night? It is the amazing grace of Jesus. "Amazing love! How can it be that thou, my God, shouldst die for me?"

7

ON JOY & HYPOCRISY

(What's Wrong with a Good Party?)

a n acquaintance approached me after church one day, disturbed by a friend of hers who appeared to her to be "leading a double life." She put it this way, "My friend is a good person. I like her a lot. But she'll go to a worship service one day, looking as holy as holy can be. And then the very next night, she's off attending a party somewhere in town, looking . . . well, not looking very holy at all. And not too worried about the contradiction that exists in her own life. I think hypocrisy is a huge problem these days. Especially among Christians. Don't you agree?"

And, of course, I shook my head and nodded in agreement. Who wouldn't? Everyone knows that the church is full of hypocrites, right? Isn't it a given that Christians—in these days or any other—would be ripe with hypocrisy? And therefore isn't it likely that her friend is just one more hypocritical Christian in a long line of fellow hypocrites through the ages?

But in retrospect, I don't think so. Not that hypocrisy isn't an important topic. And something worth thinking about, today or anytime. Nevertheless, I doubt that the underlying concern this particular person was referring to was really hypocrisy. In fact, I don't even think I see much hypocrisy on the part of Christians with whom I associate on a daily basis, nor do I think it's a major issue in the families from which most of us come or in most of the churches out of which we hail. And I'll go even further, since I'm probably already in hot water: I think genuine hypocrisy is actually quite rare today.

Now, how can I say that? And why? Don't we all know people who are leading "double lives"—going to Bible study one night and engaging in a wide range of less-than-holy activities the next? And can't we all think of people—maybe lots of them—in our home churches, or back in our home towns, who are pretending to be a certain kind of person at one moment and a different kind at another? Acting like good Christians sometimes and good pagans at others? And isn't that pretty strong evidence that I'm wrong? That hypocrisy is a real problem both in our closest circles of Christian friends and in the church at large?

I don't think so, and I'll tell you why: Hypocrisy requires a context. And that context is a culture, or a subculture at least, in which there are very clear standards of right and wrong. Where righteousness is presumed to be something one attains by doing certain things with a certain degree of frequency or intensity.

Let's take an example. What group comes to mind when you think of hypocrisy in the New Testament? The Pharisees, right? For us, the word "Pharisee" has almost become a synonym for hypocrisy. Why? Because Jesus repeatedly skewered the Pharisees for their hypocrisy, calling them "snakes," "broods of vipers," and a lot of other really nasty things. Jesus aimed his anger more frequently—and more forcefully—at the Pharisees than at any other group. The question is, what made them hypocrites? And why did Jesus get so ticked off about it?

Well, let me start off with an observation: By all accounts, Jesus, in his teaching and in his conduct, was probably more closely aligned with the Pharisees than with any other group. Surprised? Well we shouldn't be because the Pharisees were a group that tried as hard as they could to be righteous, to live according to the law of Moses—even beyond the law. They studied it with passion; they knew it with precision; and they set very high standards for themselves, trying to live out not only the details of the law but also its implications.

And Jesus was a big fan of righteousness. In fact, it's very clear that Jesus thought righteousness was every bit as important as the Pharisees did. Even more so. "Unless your righteousness *exceeds* that of the scribes and Pharisees," says Jesus, "you will never enter the kingdom of heaven" (Matthew 5:20 RSV).

Now what's going on here? Why would Jesus be so critical of a group that, theologically speaking, was quite close to him and was trying to do what he himself urged—that is, live a righteous life? The answer is hypocrisy. The Pharisees—too many of them—were using the law not as a vehicle for loving God but as a means of loving themselves.

Look at Jesus' words from Matthew 23:

> Woe to you, scribes and Pharisees, hypocrites! for you tithe mint and dill and cummin, and have neglected the weightier matters of the law, justice and mercy and faith; these you ought to have done, without neglecting the others. You blind guides, straining out a gnat and swallowing a camel! . . .
>
> You cleanse the outside of the cup and of the plate, but inside they are full of extortion and rapacity. You blind Pharisee! First cleanse the inside of the cup and of the plate, that the outside also may be clean. . . .

You are like whitewashed tombs, which outwardly appear beautiful, but within they are full of dead men's bones and all uncleanness. So you also outwardly appear righteous to men, but within you are full of hypocrisy and iniquity. (verses 23-28 RSV)

In other words, the Pharisees would promenade around Jerusalem showing off their righteousness and at the same time use the law to perpetrate injustice and fill their own purses. They were very good at pointing out the faults in others and exalting themselves in the process.

So here's the question: Do you think a modern-day Pharisee would attend a church service one night and a party the next? Not likely. In fact, a contemporary Pharisee wouldn't be caught dead partying! Instead, he would position himself prominently at the church service for all to notice and then follow it up with a front row appearance at Bible study the night after that. Indeed, he would parade down the center aisle at church to take his seat in the first pew and look deeply pious throughout the service—no doubt taking notes and making sure that everything said was biblically correct. Of course, he would be quick to point out any errors. Throughout it all, he would be putting himself on public display, in hopes that everyone would see his religiosity and admire him for his faith. And he would zealously try to get everyone else to live up to his standards, burdening them with a long list of dos and don'ts and profiting in some way as a result. But all of this would be a farce because it would not be based on a love for God but a love for himself.

Now the question is, does that ring a bell? Do you see a lot of that going on around you these days? Well, perhaps you can think of a few folks who fit into that mold, but *I* can't. I really can't. Not that I don't know people who sit in the front row at church, attend Bible studies regularly or engage teachers in discussions about biblical truth. I do, and there's nothing wrong with their behavior. It's good, in fact. They are doing these things because they are genuinely interested and want to learn. But what I don't encounter are Christians who are "advertising" their righteous activities so that everyone will notice. Why is that?

Well, I wish it were good news. I wish the answer were that we are just much better at loving God than the Pharisees were, and therefore we are much less tempted by the sin of hypocrisy. But I fear that's not the case. You'll remember that I said hypocrisy requires a context—a culture in which there are clear standards of right and wrong and a clear sense that being righteous is a good thing. Why? Because hypocrites only benefit from their hypocrisy if others envy them. Envy them for their righteousness.

In Jesus' day, one could score points by looking and acting very righteous. People would look at a good Pharisee and say, or at least think, "I wish I could do that. I wish I could be like that." Looking righteous gave them power and prestige. That's why they did it.

But here's the problem: In our day, in our culture, looking righteous doesn't bring respect, it brings ridicule. And looking pious doesn't give you power, it just looks . . . silly. I mean, can you recall observing a real straight arrow, goody-two-shoes type—who was even a bit arrogant in his or her righteousness—and envying that person? I'll bet you can't. Nor can I. We're turned off by those kinds of people. Maybe even revolted just a bit.

The people who really gain our respect in this culture are people who are marked by integrity. We love integrity, don't we? Admire it. Want it for ourselves. But what do we mean by "integrity"? Well, it turns out that, for most of us, it doesn't mean what it should mean: that is, leading an integrated life around some core of common virtues. Rather, for us integrity means "doing your own thing," living the way you want without feeling burdened by the expectations of others, being "true to yourself." In other words, for us integrity means a cultivated indifference to the needs and concerns of others in favor of devotion to one's own agenda. One's own life. One's own aspirations.

So here's the deal: In Jesus' culture, what we call "integrity" they would have termed selfishness. Or just plain sloth. Far from being admired, it would have been repudiated. In the same way, and for the same reason, what they called "hypocrisy" we call . . . what? Well, we don't call it anything, since we don't see it very often. Why would we, in a culture where there is no benefit to appearing to be righteous? Why make the effort? We are not morally alert enough either to *want* to appear righteous or to *recognize* true hypocrisy.

Real Hypocrisy

So then, what does this say about those who are leading "double lives," those who are going to worship services one night and partying till the cows come home the next? If that isn't hypocrisy, then what is it? If a person isn't trying to make others *think* he's righteous when he's really not, what *is* happening?

Let me suggest three possibilities, starting with the one that seems most likely, given the nature of modern culture: First, such conduct might result from what I would call "dulled moral sensibilities." That is, morally erratic behavior could simply stem from being morally obtuse—dense, unsharpened, unaware. Living in a moral fog, if you will.

Think of a person walking through a desert, meandering in every direction, going one way for a time and then suddenly cutting back in another. What would you conclude? Well, you'd assume that person was lost, that he had no compass, no map to guide him through uncharted territory. He lacked direction, and his behavior showed it.

In the same way, people without moral categories lack moral direction. They can't figure out which way to go because they have no moral map. They can't resist any tempting mirage on the horizon because they don't have a moral compass to tell them which way is true north. Lacking in moral *sensibilities,* in other words, they lack moral *sense.*

All of us—Christian or not—come out of a culture that struggles precisely with this issue. Indeed, that is why it's almost impossible to be a hypocrite in our culture: righteous living is not valued enough to make it worth our pretensions. And for better or for worse, Christians are products of this culture. We have been raised on its entertainment, weaned on its pleasures, fed by its amoral understandings. And it would be surprising indeed if all this food, this steady diet, didn't have some effect.

This hit home with me not long ago while I was talking with a friend, and a well-educated Christian, who was having trouble figuring out what was wrong with pornography. A regular user of the Internet, he had recently found himself exploring a range of pretty graphic, pretty sexually explicit websites. He said he found it interesting and kind of fun, and he was wondering exactly what the harm was. Wasn't it sort of a learning experience? And who was really being damaged by it anyway? He was doing it alone. No one else even knew about it. So why was it a problem?

As I listened to him, two thoughts ran through my mind. First, I understood exactly what he was saying. It seemed reasonable. His words made good sense. But second, how completely *nonsensical,* how morally bankrupt that "good sense" really was. Pornography, I had to remind myself, turns people into objects. It makes those created in God's image targets of lust. It is totally self-consuming, totally narcissistic and about as far removed from genuine love of another—and the First Commandment—as one can get. It harms those who make it; it harms those who use it, rotting souls and destroying lives all around.

But still, we have a hard time figuring out what's so bad about it. And if that's the case for a well-educated Christian—indeed, if I myself had to think about it that hard as I was listening to him—then why would we have trouble with a little praise singing on one night and a little hard partying the next? Why not? What's the problem? No big deal. No moral sense.

So moral dullness remains possibility number one for why people lead "double lives." A second possibility—and one that probably characterizes Christians to a greater degree—is that the double-minded among us are not so much morally *dull* as morally *weak*. That is, they have some moral sense, but they lack the willpower to resist temptation—lack what some would call the "courage of their convictions." And so they find it difficult to "resist" either good or evil, either a wonderful spiritual experience on one occasion or a wonderful sensual experience on the other. They are experience junkies, in other words, without the guts to "just say no" to anything.

This is a problem with which, I suspect, we can all identify. I know I have wrestled long and hard with it in my own life. And I'm quite sure that we have *all* failed in the moral courage department at one time or another. We all have our stories to tell. And we are all too embarrassed to tell them.

And if that's the case, then I say, "Good." Not good that we've failed. But good that we're embarrassed. That may not make our therapists happy, but I still think it's a good thing, nevertheless. I'm a real fan of guilt, by the way. Think it's a gift. Think most of us need more of it. I realize, of course, that sometimes we get carried away and beat ourselves silly with guilt. That's bad. Don't do it. But generally, guilt is good. And the fact that we're embarrassed by our own stories about moral lapses and don't want to share them—well, I take that as a positive sign. It means we're not back in the "morally dull" camp.

There are two things to keep in mind, I think, if you find yourself in the "morally weak" camp. First the bad news: God really *does* care about righteousness. When Jesus says, "your righteousness must surpass that of the Pharisees," he isn't kidding. This isn't hyperbole. Jesus sets a higher standard of righteousness than anyone else in the Bible. He wasn't just against adultery, he was against lust; he wasn't just against theft, he was against coveting things. Time and time again, Jesus sets the standard higher than the law. So if by chance you've grown up with the idea that Jesus is, well . . . a nice guy, and that being morally weak is, well . . . okay with him, well . . . forget it. Jesus *weeps* over our sin. And he expects his followers to live a life of deep and true righteousness.

In fact, let me go further and give you this warning: You will not long journey with Jesus if you stay among the morally weak. It just won't happen. You'll feel too uncomfortable in his presence. You won't be able to live with the guilt. And you will find yourself either drifting away from him or finding the courage to say no to what you should say no to, and yes to that to which he calls you. The double-minded Christian is not long double-minded. Or Christian.

But Jesus also understands our plight, which is the second thing to remember. He knows our weakness from the inside out. He is our brother as well as our Christ. And his understanding was so great, and his love so deep, that he went to the cross specifically for our own rescue. And he promises to equip for the journey those who desire to walk with him. He will give you the protection you need from evil; he will give you the hard knocks you need to toughen you up; and he will be there, with outstretched hand, to pull you out of the moral swamp and set you on your way. Assuming you're willing to grab the hand.

What Jesus Would Do

Finally, I think it is possible that some people find themselves at a worship service one night and a party the next, because that's exactly what Jesus might have done. And exactly what they, as followers of his, might be called to do as well. I say this cautiously and carefully, because I know it's quite possible that this statement could be used by Christians as a justification for wrongdoing, a spiritual license to sin. But if you've been with me so far, you know that's not my meaning, nor is sin anything Jesus would approve of.

What Jesus *does* sanction, and what he himself did time and time again, is to enter into the world of those he came to save. Indeed, isn't that the whole point of the incarnation? "The Word became flesh and made his dwelling among us." Among us sinners. Not to become *like* us but to *save* us from our sins. Indeed, Jesus had such a penchant for involving himself in every sector of life that he was condemned (by the Pharisees, of course) for associating himself with winebibbers, tax collectors and lowlifes of all kinds. Jesus did not avoid parties; sometimes he even sought them out.

But Jesus didn't go to parties merely to tell everyone they were going to hell. He seemed to be there, in part, because he regularly found listening ears there—people who were aware of their own moral impoverishment and were humble enough to know of their need for him. A lot more people than he ever found among the Pharisees.

Nor does it seem that Jesus was there only to preach. On one

occasion at least, he turned water into wine when the host suddenly found himself in short supply. Of course, this was a wed-
ding party, not a Saturday night bash on Main Street. And it is
clear, to me anyway, that the larger purpose of this act was to
establish his authority over creation, not to demonstrate his
ability as a vintner nor to be the life of the party. You'll notice
that John records (in John 2:11) that immediately after this miracle, "his disciples put their faith in him." They were starting to
see that Jesus was different. Nevertheless, the wine he made was
the very best wine, John tells us. And by Jesus' act, he entered
into and provided for the occasion.

So what does this mean for us? It means, first of all, that there
is no conflict between following Christ and going to a good
party or attending occasions where there are people behaving
in a less-than-holy manner. Indeed, God may lead you there.
But second, your purpose in going is not to bolster your ego, not
to prove your identity, not to score a few points, not to establish
your place in the pecking order, not to drown your sorrows, not
to make yourself look good, not to satisfy your every desire, not
to follow the crowd, not to put others down—not to do a hundred and one other things that people generally do at parties
these days, all of which focus on me and my needs, and wind up
hurting others in the process. And me, in the long run.

So why then would we ever find ourselves at a party? Well, in
the first place, it might be a good party. There *are* some, you
know. And if it is, you will find there what I call the marks of
"party good." They are love, joy, peace, patience, kindness,
goodness, faithfulness, gentleness and self-control. Against
such parties there is no law! Instead, there is fellowship—fellowship that flows not from artificial stimulation, but the pure
joy that comes from just being together. That's how God created
us. We need one another. And it is good to affirm that God-

given dimension of our humanity.

But not every party is a good one, and even at a good party not everyone there is going to be a happy camper. And for that reason, I think it is pretty likely—perhaps inevitable—that you will sometimes find there the kind of people that Jesus so often seemed to find: needy people, vulnerable people, people who are weak and aware of their own weakness. And when you do, when you encounter such people, you will have a choice to make. And everything will turn on your choice. Everything. For their need will become for you either an opportunity for their fulfillment, or for your own. And you will be for them either a source of solace or of sorcery. A listening ear or a pounding heart. The one who provides a healing touch or a touch of another kind altogether. And at that moment you will know, finally, why you are at the party. You will know why you are there and who it was that brought you. And so will all the hosts of heaven.

So how's your "party life"? Or more important, what was it like last weekend? And what will it be like on the weekends to come? If you are among the morally dull, it won't much matter, because you probably aren't reading this anyway. And even if you are, I doubt it will have much effect. But let those with ears hear: You are a walking time bomb. At some point, you're going to go off and you're going to take a lot of folks with you. In other words, you are going to have a lot to account for. And on the day of accounting, you will be dull no longer.

For the rest of us, however, I suspect the real issue is not about moral dullness but moral weakness. And the question is not, "Do we care?" but "What is the consequence of our caring?" In other words, do we have the courage to live according to our convictions, whether we're at a worship service or at a party? Whether we're in class or out of it? Whether we're

plugged into the Internet or an electric guitar? Whether someone's watching or we are doing the watching?

In other words, will we have the moral courage to do what we
know is right? The answer is important, by the way, because
your answer to that question will determine not only how you
behave, but who you are. And who you will become. And the joy
you will have in the becoming. In other words, your future
hangs in balance. And I believe all the world is hanging there
with you.

Strong statement? I don't think so. We are among the privileged of the world. We can take that privilege and party on,
dude. We won't do it for long, but we can do it. Or we can take
that privilege, those gifts, and become the people that Christ is
calling us to become.

To whom much is given, much is required. But to those who
know what they have been given, and by Whom, much is appreciated. And enjoyed. Both now and forever.

8

ON JOY & REDEMPTION

(Why Should I Benefit from Someone Else's Pain?)

Few questions are more persistent than the one we have dubbed *the problem of pain*. In Harold Kushner's words, "Why do bad things happen to good people?" But during the summer of 1999, I ran into an even more troubling question. That was the summer that Judy and I went to France with a number of good friends. We had an absolutely marvelous time. The food was great. The friends were even better. And France was just fabulous. A feast for heart, mind and soul (not to mention stomach).

One of the things that fed my soul in France was art. We focused a great deal of our time on Vincent van Gogh, who, for me up till then, was just one of a number of famous artists I knew *of* but didn't know much *about*. I knew, of course, that he was considered both to be a great artist and a bit of a crazy man. Why else would he cut off his ear? And I also knew that he painted in very large brush strokes. Beyond that, nothing much.

I found those facts interesting but didn't consider them

entirely worthy of my attention. To tell you the truth, the ear thing sort of bothered me. And frankly I worried that perhaps the art community was fascinated with van Gogh for the wrong reasons—that he was popular for his eccentricity rather than for his proficiency as an artist.

But that summer in France, I found out that I was wrong. Very wrong. And as I began to read about van Gogh and study his art and read his letters, and finally actually see van Gogh's paintings, I not only began to like his work—I did a complete 180. I loved it. And love it to this day. And I don't like it because I can read all kinds of sociological meaning into it ("Notice that the church's windows are painted dark; obviously he was struggling with the role of the church," etc.). Those kinds of observations may or may not be true. I don't know. What I *do* know for certain is that his paintings are just beautiful. As bright and vivid and compelling as any I have ever seen. They bring joy to my heart, solace to my soul.

And during the summer of 1999, it was precisely this pleasure that created a problem for me. The question was, "How can I find such pleasure in paintings that were born of such pain?" I mean, van Gogh was perfectly miserable for much of his life. And he was most productive as an artist during the time that he was in and out of mental hospitals, being spurned by friends, feeling failure at every turn and doing things like cutting off his ear. And then, as if that wasn't enough, he ended his life by suicide.

And that didn't go very smoothly either. He's the only person I know of who has gone out to a field to shoot himself and aimed so poorly that, after doing the deed, was able to walk a mile or so back home and then take another day or two to die. Let's face it, this is a pathetic story—a tragic story of a man who was haunted by his own ideals, and driven, and, to make matters worse, fairly earnest in his Christian convictions as well! Indeed, this pastor's son served as an evangelist to the poor, preaching to the workers in the coal mines in Holland and teaching about God's love to the poor and needy—all before he became an artist. And to my knowledge, there's no evidence that van Gogh ever turned away from his faith, though he clearly struggled with the church as an institution.

The point is, we're not talking about faint shadows on an idyllic life here. This is a deeply disturbing story of a man who, from all accounts, wanted to do good but was vexed from within and without, and whose life had a catastrophic conclusion. And yet he painted wonderful pictures. Wonderfully creative, wonderfully colorful, wonderfully inspiring pictures that feed the soul. And as I marveled at his paintings, I wanted to know how this could be! It certainly seemed odd to me, this strange marriage of pain and pleasure. But beyond that, it didn't seem *right* either. For me to get so much soul satisfaction from another man's pain.

Why? Well, because God is good, for one thing. The Bible teaches that from beginning to end. And both intellectually and existentially, I can affirm that God is good. So why then would things be so arranged that my pleasure would come at van Gogh's expense, out of his pain? It just doesn't seem to fit. Understand that I'm not just bringing up the proverbial problem of pain ("Why do bad things happen to good people?"). That's comparatively easy, I think. First, there are no truly good people. And second, we are the victims of one another's sin, as well as our own. Thus, bad things are going to happen. To everyone.

So I can, in some limited sense, understand the problem of pain. But this dependence of pleasure—my pleasure—on van Gogh's pain: that's the one that had me stumped and quite disheartened in France. But then something happened. Not quickly, mind you. But slowly. Over time, I started noticing something in the Bible that I had never really noticed before: My experience with van Gogh was not unique. In the Bible, at least, I began seeing the same thing happen over and over again.

It's there at the heart of the story of Israel, where, out of a people enslaved and in bondage over hundreds of years a new nation was born. Through tough times and bitter experiences God brought out, and set apart, and entered into a sacred covenant with Israel, resulting in the foundational books of the Bible and, thereby, my nurture and edification.

Or think of David's disastrous affair with Bathsheba, which led to murder and the death of their first child. Out of that pain came contrition and forgiveness, the birth of Solomon and a renewed heart in David that inspired some of the most moving poetry ever penned on parchment.

Or think of Hosea, the prophet whose wife kept cheating on him. What did Hosea do about the pain she caused him? He kept forgiving her and taking her back, at God's request. Why? So that Israel might see—and so that I might see—what it's like to be God. Through Hosea's pain, I have the joy of understanding God's faithfulness.

Or think of the other prophets—any of the other prophets—who, on the whole, lived miserable and painful lives, often in seclusion and sometimes enduring visions they themselves could hardly bear to describe. What was the point? That we might know what God has done and what God is doing and what God will do in the days to come.

Or finally, think of Jesus, the Christ, our Messiah. His parables were almost never understood. His miracles were usually misinterpreted. His associations with sinners almost always caused him grief. The religious leaders of his day were out to get him. His disciples deserted him precisely at his moment of greatest need. And his execution was the most unjustified and undeserved in all of human history. And what do we get from that? The salvation of our souls! Forgiveness! The pardon of sins and reconciliation with our Creator! In other words, the greatest of all pains resulted in the greatest of all joys. And this is the very heart of the Gospel.

Beauty from Brokenness

But why this pattern of paradox—not only for me with van Gogh, but for Israel and David and Hosea and, ultimately, Jesus himself? What's going on, anyway?

Well, I'm not entirely sure, but I think it has something to do with a silk purse. You've heard the old adage "You can't make a silk purse out of a sow's ear," I'm sure—usually thrown at someone who's trying to do the impossible—trying to turn something tired and tattered into something beautiful. And so we say, "You can't do that! You can't make a silk purse out of a sow's ear!" But God seems bent on saying, "You're wrong. I *can* do that. That's exactly what I'm in the business of doing." And basically, it's the salvage business, a grand and impossible reclamation project. And God does it all the time.

In fact, God has done that for anyone who is a follower of Jesus, has he not? That's certainly my story. And such is the experience of every other Christian I've ever known in my life. This is what the Hound of Heaven is up to, prowling around the world on all fours, waiting to pounce on new and unsuspecting people. Not to devour them. But to breathe new life into sure death. He doesn't do it on command. Nor does he lay out his plans in detail for our inspection and approval. He is God, after all. And his reclamation projects are his doing, not ours.

But we can do this: We can spot them. And rejoice in them. And we can tell our children's children about them. Reminding ourselves again that God is good. Reminding ourselves again of what he has done, and is doing, and will be doing in the days to come.

And so we Christians celebrate when good comes out of disaster, when joy comes out of pain. Because victory has been snatched from the jaws of defeat. The Evil One's plans have once again been thwarted, just when it looked as though he was on the verge of blotting out all goodness.

Think about van Gogh again for just a moment. What if, after his death, his works had been received exactly as they were during his final years as an artist? You may remember that not many people bought van Gogh's paintings before he died. A few artists recognized his talent, but many others disparaged it, especially some of those he himself admired a great deal. His work just didn't catch on as did that of other impressionists. And given that, his name, along with his work, should have just slipped away into anonymity. Another artist never to be heard of again, his paintings trashed or used as fuel to warm a cold winter's night.

But that didn't happen. Why? Well, for one thing, van Gogh had a brother, Theo, who never lost confidence in him. Theo supported Vincent financially during the latter part of his life so that he could continue to paint. He also kept Vincent's letters and worked to correct the image some had of him as a crazy man. During Vincent's life, Theo tried to sell his paintings, but when he couldn't, he kept them and treasured them. Theo was survived by his wife, another faithful figure, who hung Vincent's paintings all over her home and eventually lived to see the first glimmer of public interest in his work. All of which made it possible, one day a hundred years later, for Stan Gaede to walk into a museum and have his breath cut short, his heart filled, and his life enriched by the work of Vincent van Gogh.

That's the human story of van Gogh. And interestingly enough, it's a story of stewardship and faithfulness. Of a brother and sister who put into practice the second great commandment. But there's another story here, and it's even bigger, in my opinion. It's a story we have a hard time seeing, at the beginning of the twenty-first century, because we have put on a pair of glasses that makes it hard for us even to recognize it. But most human beings throughout the ages *have* recognized it. Even most of those who do not know about the God of Abraham, Isaac and Jacob.

In order to appreciate this story, you have to understand the flipside of the problem of pain. Let's call it the "problem of goodness." The question is, in a world of misery and injustice, how can one account for the persistent outbreaks of goodness? Why is it that even the poor experience times of joy? Why do even the most malevolent people show moments of tenderness and compassion? Why do even the sick and dying manifest times of abundant life? That, by the way, has been *the* question throughout most of human history. Not the problem of pain. Why? Most people have been poor, for one thing. Most have recognized their own failings and limitations, for another. And most have been smart enough to understand that they will get sick and die, often at an early age.

But in our culture those fairly simple facts are very hard for us to admit. We think we deserve to be rich. And indeed, compared to most in the world, we are. We think people are basically okay. We affirm each others' shortcomings as mere "differences." And we go to great lengths to deny the simple fact that we all get sick, we all age, and we all die. Never has there been a people so dedicated to the pursuit of youth and so blind to the inevitability of death.

Newsweek magazine recently ran on its cover the face of a beautiful young woman with little hand-drawn, squiggly lines around her nose, chin and cheek bones. The lines all represented places a plastic surgeon could come in and improve just a bit. And inside the edition was a lengthy feature article on all the things we are doing to our bodies at great expense to make them slightly more attractive: liposuction, nose jobs, implants, injections—you name it, we've tried it. Do we have more money than brains, or what? I mean, what in the world are we doing? Now I'm not complaining here that we want to improve our looks—that's very human. I'm not complaining about plastic surgeons either; I was in an automobile accident at age nineteen that smashed half my jaw. If it weren't for the artistic ability of a very capable surgeon, I would be a very different-looking fellow today. And I am grateful.

What seems odd to me is not that we want to improve our looks, but that we fool ourselves into thinking we can control the future. Put off the inevitable. Which is why, when the inevitable comes, we get really ticked off. When we don't get rich as planned. When we are treated unjustly. When we or others get sick, or die at an early age. At those times we moderns rail against God and say, "How can you let bad things happen to good people?"

But the people of any other culture, at any other time, would ask us: "What do you mean? Why did you assume everything would be wonderful? And how on earth did you miss the fact the you are going to get sick and die?" You see, the question isn't, "Why do bad things happen to good people?" The question is, "Why do good things happen at all?" Why, in the face of the reality of death, do we continue to believe in and enjoy life?" It is clearly the problem of goodness that we face. And that has led human beings throughout the ages to seek answers beyond themselves. In something bigger and grander than this pitiful life to account for it.

Of course, followers of Jesus know exactly why there are outbreaks of goodness: because the God who created everything, including us, is good. And in spite of our own rebellion, our own sin, God will not allow his goodness to be defeated. His goodness is irrepressible, even though the prince of darkness still has his say, and his dominion, in this world. But his doom is sure. Why? Because of Jesus. Because "God was pleased to have his fullness dwell in him, and through him [through Christ] to reconcile to himself all things, whether things on earth or things in heaven, by making peace through his blood, shed on the cross" (Colossians 1:19-20).

That's what God has done and is doing and will be doing in the days to come. And so to remind us of that fact God periodically confounds the course of human events to expose beauty and goodness in the most unlikely places for all the world to see. And that is what he did, I think, with van Gogh. He took a roller coaster that was absolutely off its track and heading into the abyss and completely turned it around. For whom? Well, not for van Gogh—in this life anyway. Van Gogh didn't see it happen. No, God did it for us. For our pleasure. He redeemed van Gogh's life for us, using the faithful efforts of two faithful people.

Why do I get such pleasure out of art that was born of pain and sorrow? Because our God is the great Redeemer. Who will not allow evil to triumph. Who does not leave well enough alone. And every time we celebrate the wonder of a work of art or the beauty of a grand symphony or the poignancy of a poem born of pain, we declare: Our God is an awesome God, who is good. And he will not be defeated!

9

ON JOY & CAREER
(Why Can't I Play Third Base?)

a while back I served on a search committee to fill a pastoral position at the church we were attending. As is often the case, we were interviewing lots of candidates. And I was having a great time because I was getting to hear all kinds of stories about how God had worked in the lives of lots of people who had lots of stories worth hearing.

In the middle of one of the interviews, a particular candidate—who had already enjoyed a successful career in a variety of church ministries—began sharing his struggles about his calling into the ministry. What fascinated me about his story was the contrast between his outward success as a pastor and his inner struggle with his calling. On the one hand, he had had phenomenal success since going into the ministry: his churches grew, he saw people come to Christ and grow in their faith, and he was surrounded with people who sang his praises. Yet deep within his heart he really struggled with whether or not he was in the right spot—whether he was hearing God's call correctly.

Now on the surface, this seemed pretty odd to me: Why all this evidence of success and, at the same time, all these doubts? Why didn't he just accept the fact that he was good at his work, that God was blessing him in it, and live at peace with himself? Of course, if I had thought a little harder I would have realized that this is often the case: that success is sometimes fueled by self-doubt and sometimes breeds it as well. But I wasn't thinking that hard at the time, and so I just sat there kind of puzzled as I listened to his story.

Finally, someone on the committee went from curiosity to candor and asked Mike the question we were all thinking: "Why all these self-doubts when you are obviously so good at what you do?" And then, as if on cue, he began telling us about his conversion experience, which occurred during his college years and which absolutely turned his life around. He said he had no doubt from that moment on that he wanted to give his life to Christ, to follow him wherever it might lead.

He was, however, a very good athlete. In fact, he was in college on an athletic scholarship, and his coach and others had told him that he had the potential to be a professional baseball player. The question that immediately hit him, therefore, was whether his new life in Christ meant that he should continue on in athletics or pursue some other career. And so he did what lots of people do at such times—he sought advice from those he most admired, and one of them was a leader at the church he was then attending.

As it turns out, this church leader wasn't shy about offering advice. He told him, in no uncertain terms, that he should go into full-time Christian work and that his next destination should be seminary, not a baseball diamond. "Mike," he said with all the force of a general giving orders, "let some pagan play third base! You're being called into the ministry, not baseball." And that's what Mike did. He went into the pastorate. And he was successful. And on the whole he was glad he did. But he still struggled with his calling, and he didn't know why.

But I did. And so did everyone else sitting there around the table that day. Once we'd heard the story of the advice Mike had received as an early convert, we knew exactly why he was struggling.

And we were also pretty confident we knew what he should do about it: he should go back to that church leader who told him to "Let some pagan play third base," and tell the fellow to stop giving so much advice. And start studying his Bible a bit more carefully. Especially the beginning. About creation. And God's intentions concerning the world he created.

In fact, the more I thought about his story, the more I fumed. "Let some pagan play third base?" I mumbled to myself. "And why not let some pagan write all our novels, too! And let some pagan produce our movies. And let some pagan run our businesses. And let some pagan do our scholarship, and study the stars, and tell us about our history. And let some pagan create our music. And let some pagan produce our art. And let some pagan shape our politics. And let some pagan define our social problems. And let some pagan treat our diseases. And let some pagan run our colleges and universities. In other words, let the pagans do all of the things that God created us to do in the first place! I mean, what kind of philosophy was this, not to mention theology!" I thought. And it ticked me off.

And it still does, as you can tell. Not only because it's bad advice. But because it strikes at the heart and soul of what we have been called to be and do as followers of Jesus Christ. And the problem wasn't that the church leader told this fellow he should be a pastor—that's a very important vocation. We need pastors, especially good ones, and by all accounts Mike turned out to be a good pastor. The problem wasn't even the arrogance of the advice, presuming as he did to know Mike's calling better than Mike himself did. That's possible, of course. Perhaps he had the gift of discernment.

The real problem was that, in the way he delivered his advice, he privileged one role over another. And, in the process, assumed that our work in the *world* is somehow inferior—less valuable—than our work in the church. At the most basic level, that's bad advice. Biblically wrong, to be blunt. But practically speaking, it takes the world that God created and called good and turns it over to those who don't know that. Or more to the point, it asserts that we who are Christians are in the singular business of sharing our faith and teaching one another, not in the business of living out our faith and practicing it in the world in which God placed us.

Going Where God Calls

Our calling to follow Christ isn't a call *out* of the world, however, but *into* it. God loves the world he created. He grieves over the fact that we have rebelled against him and his plan for us to be good stewards of his world. And so he sent Christ, in order that we who follow him might become new creations—those who seek to live according to the way God created us in the first place, to be the good stewards we should have been all along. And that means entering into every kind of job, every kind of role, every kind of occupation, and redeeming it—working at it as new creations who employ transformed minds and renewed hearts, and performing all these tasks the way we should have from the beginning.

And that includes playing third base, by the way. If that's how God has gifted you. And if that's what he has called you to. It also includes full-time missions—going to another culture for a lifetime, if that's what your call implies, and sharing the good news of Jesus Christ so that others might be new creations in their work as well. And it includes becoming a chemist. Or a farmer. Or a scholar. Or a physician. Or a parent. Or some combination of the above.

But it absolutely does *not* imply the preferring of one task over another. Listen to what Paul says in 1 Corinthians 12: "There are *varieties* of gifts, but the same Spirit. And there are *varieties* of ministries, and the same Lord. And there are *varieties* of effects, but the same God who works *all things* in all persons. . . . There are many members, but one body. . . . You are Christ's body, and *individually* members of it" (verses 4-6, 20, 27 NASB, emphasis added).

Remember Eric Liddell, the Scotsman who ran for his country in the 1924 Olympics? If you've seen the movie *Chariots of Fire* you know that the issue we're talking about here is precisely the one that Eric Liddell struggled with (in the movie, anyway) as he tried to figure out whether he should be an athlete or a full-time missionary. Actually, it was more his sister's struggle and the struggle of others in his family who felt he was called to share the gospel around the world. And of course they were right. But the problem was, as Eric himself said, "God also made me fast." And then, in one of the finest lines in the history of "moviedom" he declared, "When I run I feel God's pleasure."

He said that to his sister when she was pleading with him to give up running and go into full-time missionary work. And every time I see that scene I want to say, "Amen, Eric! Preach it, brother! Of course you feel God's pleasure! That's how God created you!" You see, the heavens rejoice when God's creatures honor their Creator with the gifts and abilities he has given them. Why? Because that was his original plan. And it is still God's plan for us—today and in the world to come. It's the rea-

son liberal arts colleges like mine exist, by the way: to develop
and sharpen our God-given gifts and abilities so that we might
flourish, becoming the people God created us to be. And it's
what all parents want of their children as well, if they are followers of Jesus. To hear God's call, to follow and to feel God's pleasure in the midst of it.

"But what does that mean specifically for me?" That's the
question, right? And it's hard to avoid even if you want to. After
all, you have to make decisions at every turn that to a certain
degree will set the course for your future. College. First job. And
then a second, or perhaps a third. To move, or not to move. To
graduate school, or not to graduate school. So how do you make
these decisions? And where will you find your joy?

Well, I can tell you definitively: I don't know. And my guess is
that no one around you knows either. I'm guessing that just
based on the evidence, by the way. None of the original twelve
disciples knew where Christ's call would take them when they
were going to school with Jesus. Not one. Their experience of
following Jesus was just one huge surprise after another. And
that's the norm.

Take a quick stroll through the Bible and find there the number of people who knew early on where God was calling them.
You will find a few—very, very few. The vast majority were
rather astonished about where God led them, and I suspect we
will be too. The reality is, God does not give us the full picture of
what he has in mind for our lives from beginning to end. He
gives us glimpses at times but not the full picture. Most of the
time he simply says, "Follow me today. Honor me today. Love
me and your neighbor today. And trust me for the future." But
where will that future take you? I don't know.

But here's what I do know: Right now, if you are a follower of
Christ, you are up to something. And that something is part and

parcel of your calling. If you are a parent, that's part of your calling. Guaranteed. If you're an accountant or an athlete or an artist—that's your calling as well, for today, at least. And if you're in college or graduate school, you are called to be a student. For now. And as you throw yourself into the task of learning or art or child rearing, you ought to "feel God's pleasure," as Eric Liddell put it. And when you do, the heavens will rejoice.

The Rest of the Story
But where you are today probably won't be the end of your story. You will be called to someplace else, no doubt, to do other things in God's good time and for his good pleasure—just as Eric Liddell was called someplace else after he won his Olympic gold medal. And that's the part of Eric's story that the movie leaves out. It hints at it at the end. But by and large what you're left thinking about at the end of *Chariots of Fire* is the success that Eric had at the Olympics, both on and off the track. Success in sticking to his principles. And success in sticking it to everyone else on the track.

But there's more to the story of Eric Liddell—a lot more—and I learned about it a few years ago while reading a book that a friend recommended to me. The book was not about Eric Liddell, actually, but about a small group of people who were confined to an internment camp in China during World War II. They were mostly Westerners who were living in China at the outbreak of the war and who had gotten caught behind Japanese lines when the latter overran China. As a result, they were put in a camp called Shantung Compound, where they had to live together on meager rations and not much hope for the future.

Now the reason my friend recommended this book to me is that I'm a sociologist, and this book is actually a reflection on community—or more precisely, a study of human nature and the moral community. The author is Langdon Gilkey, now a retired scholar at the University of Chicago—but he wasn't at the time the story takes place. In fact, he was one of the people trapped in the internment camp; he himself was one of the prisoners. And he wrote this book because his experience there completely changed his view of human beings. He went to China as a young teacher fresh out of Harvard, assuming that human beings are basically good. But he left the camp knowing absolutely that humans beings are not good—at least, not when left to their own devices and instincts.

But toward the end of the book he begins talking about one person in the camp who was different. Who was good. His name was Ridely—Eric Ridely. He says that Ridely was about as close to a saint as anyone he'd ever met in his life. For example, the teenagers in the camp apparently had an especially difficult time of it, with too much freedom on their hands and nothing to do. And so they got into increasingly more trouble and at one point were holding what, in the opinion of the adults, were something close to orgies—secret meetings where abominable things were happening. No one knew quite what to do about it. Rules didn't work. Nothing worked. And the grown-ups were at their wits' end.

But then something rather unexpected occurred. Eric Ridely decided to give himself to these young people. He stayed with them all the time, organized sporting events and games for them, did a little teaching and anything else he could to befriend and love them. And all of a sudden the "orgies" stopped. A whole different mood and purpose settled over the teenagers—and the camp as a whole. "If ever there was a saint," said the author, "it was Eric Ridely."

But Ridely's story does not have a happy ending. Just before the prisoners were rescued from the camp by the Allies only days before the end of World War II, Ridely died of a brain tumor. Everyone in the camp mourned. And all of Scotland mourned as well. Because, as it turns out, the saintly Eric Ridely was really . . . Eric Liddell, the Scotsman who had won in the Olympics twenty years before, the one who felt God's pleasure when he ran.

What did Eric Liddell do after he won the gold medal? Well, he kept on following Jesus, that's what he did. Just as he had done when he trained for the Olympics and outran all of his opponents. And this time, following Jesus took him to China, where he became a long-term, full-time missionary spreading the Good News until he was trapped in an internment camp and died of a brain tumor at much too early an age.

But that's not the right way to say it, is it? Because Eric Liddell was a missionary long before he went to China. He gave witness to the good news when he ran in the Olympics. He gave witness to the good news when he continued on in his missionary role and went to China to teach. And he gave witness to the good news by loving those teenagers in the internment camp; by doing what no one else was willing to do . . . or knew how to do. He heard Christ's call as clearly in an obscure camp in a remote part of China as he did in front of thousands of people at the Olympics twenty years before. And in both places, I guarantee, he felt God's pleasure. And the heavens rejoiced.

And that's what the rest of us should expect as well. On the details—on precisely where God will take you in the days ahead—I haven't a clue. It might be to play third base or pastor a church. It might be to teach at a college in your hometown or teach a farmer how to rotate crops in a far-off country. It might mean, as it did for Eric Liddell, winning the Olympic gold medal and then spending the rest of your life in obscurity, and in your last days helping a few teenagers stay out of trouble in an internment camp.

The only guarantee is this: Saying "Yes, I will follow," will take you *into* the world, not out of it. Why? Because the world belongs to God, that's why. Every square inch of it. It is his! He created it. Giving it up to the "pagans" is exactly what the Evil One hopes you will do. Reclaiming it for its Creator is exactly what the Holy One expects you to do.

If you love him, you will love his world and serve him in it. And feel God's pleasure.

10

ON JOY & HAPPINESS
(Questioning Homosexuality)

I'll be the first to acknowledge that the questions swirling around the issue of homosexuality are multiple and complex, and no scholar trained in just one area can adequately address them all. There are theological questions, political questions, philosophical questions, biological questions, and social and psychological questions—numerous questions that are, in themselves, far beyond the pale of any one individual's expertise, and certainly beyond my own.

But that's only the beginning, because this is also a deeply personal issue, one that touches some of the core concerns of our lives: dealing with identity, meaning and truth—all of which we care about passionately and are not about to let go of easily. In other words, this issue is close to our nerves. And in my experience, when that is the case defenses go up and learning is very, very difficult. So why am I talking about it?

Well, perhaps it's my sense that despite all these problems we *need* to talk about it. Perhaps it's my suspicion that there is a lot of misinformation floating around that people are quickly grabbing hold of to buttress their own opinions. But more than that, I am also convinced that if we wish to understand what the joyful life means for the Christian, then this is an issue worth taking on. Indeed, precisely because it is difficult it offers us a window into the question of happiness like none other in our day.

For starters, I should probably say that I don't believe the difficulty we face in dealing with the issue of homosexuality is due to the fuzziness of moral boundaries or the power of our natural urges. Rather, I believe it is due to the history we have inherited and the cultural context in which we live. Let me explain.

For most of us, our angst about homosexuality is predicated upon the assumption that it really is hard to figure out what's right and wrong in this area. And if you have a friend who's struggling with homosexuality, or if you yourself are dealing with this matter, my guess is that you have thought long and hard about the moral dimension of this issue. You have perhaps asked yourself, "What does Scripture teach about homosexuality? Is it really wrong to practice it in all circumstances? What if someone has grown up with a homosexual disposition—is it right for him or her to be excluded from sexual intimacy for that reason alone? Isn't it something he feels because of who he is? Would God really want her to abstain from expressing a desire that he himself has allowed her to have?" In short, isn't the moral picture pretty fuzzy when you think about this thing carefully? Or better yet, when you wrestle with it personally, either on your own behalf or on behalf of someone else?

Good questions. And they are worth wrestling with, in this day or any other. And I'll go one step further. If you haven't wrestled with them and felt the power of those questions, then you probably aren't dealing very lovingly, or very candidly, with yourself or your neighbor. This is not merely the stuff of bull sessions and scholarly debate. It is also the stuff of personal anguish. And until you have held someone in your arms and cried through these questions, well . . . you might want to be careful about answering them too quickly, because when these questions are enfleshed in a living, breathing human being, and when you love your neighbor as yourself, these questions are difficult.

Nevertheless, I do not believe what makes these questions hard is moral ambiguity. What makes them hard is history. And culture. Let me explain. First, I think we need to admit that we live with a history of pretty poor decision-making when it comes to those who have struggled with the issue of homosexuality. We have been quicker to label than to understand. We have been more interested in distancing ourselves than in bridging the gap. And we have too often dehumanized rather than identi-fied. In other words, we have had a hard time dealing with this issue with the same degree of fairness and equanimity we accord other moral issues. We have singled it out, and as a result some pretty awful things have been done in the name of truth and righteousness—in the church and outside of it. So we live today in the shadow—and with the consequences—of that his-tory.

But a sorry history is not all we live with, as some would like to believe. We also live, at present, with a culture that has a very difficult time with moral boundaries of any kind. Let's face it, we simply do not know how to define "the good" in this society any more. About the best we can come up with is that people shouldn't do anything that might offend or physically harm someone else. What this really means is that each individual is supposed to define right and wrong for himself or herself, and above all not tell anyone else what to do. In the Old Testament, a common descriptor of morally bankrupt society is "Everyone did what was right in his own eyes." But to *us*, that doesn't sound half bad, because it's about as close as we can get to any agreement on personal morality.

That's not the whole story, though, because we also hold another assumption—an ally to the first—which is that no one should ever be denied anything that she really wants or thinks she needs. In fact, we think denial is a great tragedy, don't we— whether what we want is a material object, an experience or another human being. Of course, we reluctantly accept the fact that we can't have everything we want—we understand limited resources. But what we can't abide, or even understand, is the possibility that there might be some things out there that are available to us, but that we should not have for moral reasons. That just doesn't compute.

Now the question is, what does this do for us, or to us, when we come to an issue such as homosexuality? Well, in the first place, if we understand our history and we care about people, then we are likely to feel guilty—deeply guilty—about how we have treated our brothers and sisters in the past. And that's probably not a bad thing. Guilt has its place. We ought to feel guilty for wrong behavior. And if that, in turn, makes us a little cautious about making quick judgments, that's probably good as well. Being slow to judge and quick to listen are characteristics that followers of Christ ought to be known for and marked by.

But here's the problem: When this guilt is accompanied by what is considered proper compassion in our culture, we sud- denly go from being "slow to judge" to being totally incapable of moral discernment altogether. Why? Because we don't know how to answer questions of right and wrong, remember? What we do believe is that everyone has a right to his or her own opinion. And what we feel in our gut is that it is an awful thing for any of us to communicate anything to anyone that implies any kind of moral judgment. It just *feels* bad. And so we become not just slow to speak, but absolutely speechless on matters of personal morality. And we conclude that, gosh, who knows what's really right or wrong here? It's a tough call. This is a fuzzy area.

But you know—and here you should do your own research and not just take my word for it—I really don't think this is a fuzzy area at all. Not if you take Scripture seriously. Not if you are inclined to ask, "What does Scripture really teach?" rather than, "What do I want it to teach?" And especially not if you distance yourself from the assumptions of our age regarding the priority of the self and the assumed tragedy of denial.

Indeed, one of the really striking things about this dispute in the church is what a very modern flavor it has to it. Sometimes people will say, "Well, the church changed its mind on slavery and the role of women. It will eventually change its mind on homosexuality as well." Stated that way, in the swirl of today's confusion, that statement packs a punch. But looked at historically it's a strange conclusion indeed. Why? Because questions about how to handle slavery and the roles of men and women were already evident in the New Testament and in the early church right from the start. You have Christians *freeing* slaves at the same time the latter are being encouraged to *submit* as slaves; and you have women *teaching* and *serving as deacons* at the same time that they are being admonished to *hold their tongues* in the assembly—in church. In other words, the early Christians were trying to figure out right from the start what the Gospel implied in these two important arenas of economics and male-female roles. And we continue to work on those today, with good reason.

But what the writers of the New Testament were *not* wrestling with was any moral ambiguity about proper sexual relations. It's just not there. Their writings assume from the get-go that the proper place for sex is in marriage between a husband and wife. Period. Now be careful—don't misunderstand me here. Restricting sex to this relationship *was* a problem in the early church, as it has been throughout human history. And the teachings of Christ and the letters that now make up the New Testament clearly reveal the need to remind the hearer and the reader constantly of the importance of fidelity, as well as of biblical standards of sexuality. But the need then was for reminders, not revisions—reminders about what they already knew and what was clearly taught, from beginning to end, in the biblical record. You'll find no seemingly incompatible statements about the issues of adultery, sexual promiscuity or homosexuality here.

What makes the current controversy different, then, is not some new insight into Scripture but some very new assumptions in our culture. And the key assumption is that feelings are a priori in moral considerations; that is, we think our feelings about one another should determine how we treat one another. Isn't that right? If you feel in love with someone, you sleep with them; that is the assumption of our age. And it is very hard indeed, under such an assumption, to argue that people should deny themselves sexual fulfillment—whether homosexual or heterosexual—on the basis of moral categories alone. Why? Because the moral categories are suspect. They are thwarting our feelings of happiness, and therefore they must be wrong.

Looking for Happiness

Let me tell you a story about a friend. It's a true story, but I'll call him John. He and his wife, Jennifer, became some of Judy's and my closest companions during the first decade of our marriage.

For a while, John and I were attending the same university, pursuing different degrees but the same Lord, and trying to do the right thing—or trying to figure out what "right" meant at that time and place.

That was no easy task even then, by the way. In the name of "peace, love, and happiness," some of our peers were tripping out on LSD, occupying faculty and administrative offices, and practicing communal living. All in all, that didn't sound like "peace, love, and happiness" to us, even though we were, at points, sympathetic to their cause. And so we walked a fine line between sympathy and participation, understanding and undertaking. And significantly, we walked that line together.

As we continued our education, however, our paths took us in different directions, John going one way to pursue a degree in clinical psychology, while I went back east to continue on in sociology. Our paths departed in other respects as well, however. The focus of John's work became marriage and family counseling, and he got caught up in some of the more trendy notions of the day.

Complicating the matter, he and Jennifer began having serious marital problems. Actually, "began" is not quite the right word, since John and Jen had always had their struggles. They were different in personality and temperament, and those differences both attracted them to one another and exasperated them about one another. And you would find them, on alternate days, madly in love ... or just plain mad.

As John continued his studies, things really started going downhill. And eventually, with the encouragement of his own therapist, he decided that it would be best for them to separate for awhile. Jen, who was not too pleased with some of John's trendy ideas, agreed, and within a short time their marriage was on the verge of collapse. John began experimenting with more

than just therapy. And Jennifer was not in the mood to be forgiving. Their marriage seemed doomed.

It was about that time that I got a call from Greg, a mutual
friend who was also concerned about John and Jen's marriage.
Greg said he wanted the three of us—John, Greg and me—to
go fishing together. I said, "What? I don't fish. And I don't live
in California any longer. And I don't get it."

Greg said, "Shut up. We're not doing this for you. John loves
to fish. He's coming back to California in a few weeks, and so
are you. So while you're here, I think it would be a good idea for
the three of us to go up into the High Sierras and fish. And talk.
John needs it. And so do we."

Well, what was I going to do? I was stuck. Reluctantly, then, I
agreed, knowing that I would be heading to the mountains with
two expert fishermen—and knowing too that my biggest catch
in a lifetime of fishing was a two-inch tadpole that accidentally
got stuck on my hook when I was in the second grade. And I
wasn't even fishing at the time!

But within a few weeks, I found myself at six thousand feet
staring at a lake absolutely teaming with bass—all of which
were practically jumping into John's and Greg's pockets. In fact,
all over the lake fish were leaping into the air begging to be
caught, while calm, discerning fishermen were saying, "No. No.
No. Yes, I'll take you. No . . ." It was a fisherman's paradise—
except around me, where it was still life. Christmas Eve. Not a
creature was stirring.

Of course, that evening we built a fire, cooked "our" fish, and
ate and ate and ate. It was fabulous. And disgusting. And pretty
much what Greg had hoped for all along.

In due time, fishermen do talk—not during the day while
fishing, not while preparing the fire or cooking the fish, and
certainly not while eating . . . but afterward. When the night air

is crisp and quiet, and the stars are thick as sugar, and nothing much exists but you, your thoughts, your Creator.

John started it. Started talking about what went wrong with his marriage. He talked about a marriage that was hard from the beginning, where harmony was the exception and discord a daily event. He talked about little things that irked him, big things that shattered him and everyday events that just plain wore him down.

He also talked about a colleague in graduate school who had nurtured him and counseled him and offered him more than advice. "This happens all the time, John," she told him. "Don't worry too much about it. You've grown beyond your wife. You need to move on. This experience will actually help you become a better counselor. It's time to grow up and get real. The two of you just aren't good for each other."

And John had concluded that she was right. "You know," he said in a deeply painful tone, "I don't think I can ever be really happy with Jen. We're just too different. There's no real satisfaction. I'm just not happy."

Silence followed those words, and I thought, "What can I say? John's absolutely right. He and Jen *are* different. They've been in conflict since day one. He's not happy; she's not happy. Maybe he should pursue another relationship. Maybe a little fulfillment outside his marriage is just what the doctor ordered."

But Greg was not silent, and he burst into our pity party with two of the most memorable words I have ever heard: "So what?" he said softly. "So what? You say, John, you don't think you could ever be completely happy with Jen. Well, so what? What makes you think your happiness is all that matters? Why isn't your word, your vow, more important than your happiness? Why isn't Jen more important than your satisfaction? And why, oh why, oh why," he said—not speaking to John anymore, but prophesying to the stars—"why in the world can't we live with discomfort any more these days? I mean, are we called to escape painful relationships, or reclaim them? Are we supposed to flee hurting marriages, or redeem them? Did Jesus say, throw off your cross and do your own thing, or take up your cross and follow me?"

Well, there was a moment I'll never forget. And frankly, I didn't know what in the world was going to happen next. But the world had nothing to do with it. It was a moment witnessed in this life only by three fishermen (well, two fisherman plus one), but it was seen and heard throughout the courts of heaven. In fact, I think it was number one at the box office in Paradise. I think Gabriel said, "Hush. Listen. Something important is happening here." And all heaven cocked its ear to hear John's reply.

And John said . . . not a thing. At least, nothing that we could hear. But heaven heard, I'll tell you that. Because, you see, John went home and redeemed his marriage. Asked Jen for forgiveness. Vowed again his faithfulness. And this time, John lived according to his vow.

An Uneasy Redemption

Now, why did I tell you this story? It's not about homosexuality. And it didn't even have a happy ending, if that means living in bliss forever after. John and Jen's marriage did not immediately turn around. It got better, that's for sure. And today, they are as close and loving as any two people we know. But for many years, they continued to struggle. There were many very difficult moments. They were, after all, still the same different personalities, and they still wrestled with the same issues and temptations.

But what did happen, and what I believe needs to be noted, is how God used this struggle in John's life, not for *his* benefit but for the benefit of others. You see, John went on to become a counselor, working with alcoholics and eventually developing one of the most successful and effective treatments for alcoholism there is today. How did he do it? Well, John is talented, that's part of it. But John also knows something about addiction, about craving and about denial. John knows how to tell the truth in love. and how to live accordingly. In biblical language, John knows something about the cross and about redemption.

You see, the question that we face in this area of sexuality is not about each of our own unique struggles and cravings—because we've all got them. Every one of us will at some time in his or her life confront the craving to find satisfaction with someone we should not. Every one of us. The temptation will be harder to resist for some than for others. And the distribution of pain in this area will not be fair. You may end up single all your life and find it fairly easy; but others will find it very hard. You may be married for only a short time and find it deeply satisfying; others will have life-long marriages characterized mostly by struggle, not satisfaction—sexual or otherwise. You may find yourself deeply and passionately attracted to someone you are not married to. Nor can you be. Nor should you be. And that will always be hard. I tell you right now, with all sincerity, there is nothing easy about any of this. Nothing easy.

"But . . . ," to quote the soft, clear voice of Greg in the High Sierras, "so what?" So what? Are you in this thing for ease, or is there something more at stake? You know, we say we are followers of Jesus Christ, and yet I fear that we crave a life almost in opposition to the one he lived. We want what's easy; he chose what's hard. We want life for ourselves; he chose to give his life for others. We want approval for our *own* deeds; he chose to do the deeds of his father in heaven. We seek the condemnation of others who are not like us; he wants to redeem us all.

I guess the question is, do you think Jesus was on to something here, or did he make a mistake? When it comes to the redemption part we certainly don't think he made a mistake, do we. That part we like. It's getting there that we don't like. You see, between us and the joy of redemption is the cross in all its ghastly glory. And it is, as it was then, either a stumbling block or a cornerstone of the good life.

Jesus says to take up our cross and follow him, and he will give us life. (See Luke 9:23-24.) Not easy life . . . but abundant life. Not painless life . . . but life worth living. Not joy just for today . . . but forever. With him.

11

ON JOY & WORSHIP
(A Question of Attendance)

Over a decade ago, a student came up to me after class one day and blurted out, "Dr. Gaede, why in the world do we have required chapel at this institution anyway?" Without much hesitation, and without much grace either, I blurted back, "I don't know. . . . Why do we have to eat?" And then, while my student stood there scratching his head and looking at me as though I were from Mars, I bid him farewell and walked back to my office.

I have always regretted that conversation. Not because of what I said, but for the way I said it. And also because of what I did immediately thereafter: I walked away. I gave a quick answer to an important question and then just left. And my student did not get the conversation he deserved. So here I want to make amends of sorts and re-enter that same conversation. Because the question was not really about required chapel. It was about worship. And joy. And I have come to believe that, for the Christian in pursuit of happiness, it's one of the more important questions of our time.

What Happens When We Gather

A few years ago, I lost a very close friend by the name of Gerry Davie. If I were still in high school, I'd say Gerry was my "best friend." I'm too old for that now, and I have too many good friends to be able to single out just one. But he was a friend of over twenty years. And though he and his family had moved away from us—and had continued relocating in distant parts—we kept in touch and remained very close.

The funny thing about our friendship was that Gerry and I were different in many ways. We rarely agreed about politics, for example. And our jobs were quite different: He was a successful businessman, while I kept my nose in the books as a student and a scholar. But our families loved each other, and we loved each other as well. And most important, we both loved the same Lord. And about him—about Jesus—Gerry and I could talk forever. We shared what he was doing in our lives . . . and not doing. We talked about what was *right* in the eyes of the Lord . . . and what wasn't. In other words, we did a lot of pondering about what it means to honor him with our lives in these days, in these times. I cherished those conversations. And through the years, Gerry taught me a lot about what it means to be a follower of Jesus Christ—as a husband, a father, a neighbor, a friend.

But then it all came to a screeching halt. Gerry died after battling cancer for a short year and a half. And this person on whom I had leaned for wisdom and support was gone. Death always raises lots of questions, but especially so when it's the death of someone close, and especially when it seems premature. Those questions were first raised for me at age seventeen when a friend died in Vietnam. They came again at the age of thirty when my father passed away. And they continue to bubble up to the surface again every time I lose someone to the hand of death. Whether it's a teenage friend or a middle-aged Gerry Davie, it doesn't really matter: a death, especially a premature death, just seems . . . well, obscene.

But what overwhelmed me at Gerry's death was not the unanswered questions, or even the pain of death itself, but the suffocating sense of loss—of losing a friend forever. Death separates us from the ones we love. It cuts through our assumed world of relationships—those people whom we take so for granted that we hardly bat an eye when we hurt them—and screams at us: *Fragile! Handle with care! Not forever!* And when we come face-to-face with that reality, and our own stupidity at ever thinking otherwise, we are left feeling very much alone.

Which is how I felt when I said my last goodbye to Gerry on a Thursday night as he lay dying on a hospital bed in Portland, Maine. The feeling deepened on Friday morning when his daughter, Susan, called and told us that Gerry was gone. And it continued to haunt me through the weekend and right up until we gathered together for Gerry's funeral on Monday at noon in a quaint New England church.

But then something happened. And something changed. What happened? Well, a multitude of those who had known and loved Gerry gathered together—that's what happened. In one place, at one time, in the name of the One God, we gathered together to celebrate one very generous gift to us.

We came from all over the country—some by corporate jet from Chicago, and some by private jalopy from just down the road. We were friends and neighbors, family members and business associates. We were teachers and preachers, farmers and builders, employed and unemployed. The person who had led Gerry to the Lord in the first place was there. A number were there who had learned the good news through Gerry at some point thereafter. We came. We sang. We prayed. We cried. We talked. We listened. But most of all, we gave glory to God, who created Gerry in the first place, who blessed him with the grace of Jesus Christ and blessed the rest of us in the process.

That's what *happened* on Monday at the funeral. So what *changed*? What changed as a result of that service? Well, *I* did, for one. I came to the service broken, defeated and alone; but I left knowing absolutely that I was not. Had all my questions been answered? No. Had all the pain been taken away? Certainly not. But the service on Monday had confronted me with a reality far more profound than the one I experienced the Friday before and ultimately far more genuine than anything I could have found on my own.

Death is not the final reality, that's the simple truth I learned (again) on Monday. And for the saints, eternity will not be like what I experienced all alone on Friday after Gerry's death. It will be like Monday noon, when all the saints come together to celebrate what God has done on our behalf. That's the future. And that's the reality about which we need to be continually reminded.

Reminders of Reality
Why do we gather together for worship on a regular basis? Because reality isn't what we think it is. It isn't Friday morning after Gerry's death. It isn't how you feel after you've lost a job or been dumped by a friend. Nor, for that matter, is it how you feel after you've landed a job or a promotion or a friend. Ultimate reality—the reality of the future—is not about you alone doing or being anything.

For the saints—for those who follow Jesus—ultimate reality is tasted when we come together, when God's people gather in all their diversity, from every nation and every tribe, to honor and glorify him. That's reality. You or me on our own—that's hell. You and I together with all the saints—that's heaven. And every once in a while, because God is gracious and prone to give us what we need rather than what we deserve, we're going to see a bit of that heaven reflected when we gather together with other Christians in a particular place, at a particular time. And wherever we are on the globe, whatever our circumstances, whatever our differences in taste, friends, or politics—gathering together as Christians reminds us of whose we are, and whose we shall be, forever.

That's the most important thing I can say about worship. And, unfortunately, the most difficult to remember. You see, we come to this issue of "institutionalized worship"—whether it's at church or retreat, college or retirement home—with all kinds of questions, don't we? Why can't we sing praise songs instead of traditional hymns? Why don't we use an organ instead of a guitar? Why do the pastors at some churches wear robes and others don't? Why do some churches use a pulpit and others don't? We come with a long list of questions, all of them good and important on their own, but all of which we use to delude ourselves into thinking that worship is about us. Our happiness. Our joy. And when they don't "produce," we move along. Perhaps to another church. Or perhaps to no church at all.

Which means that, deep down, we don't really believe that we need church—we don't need corporate worship. We've got things to do, places to go, people to see. Until one day we wake up and discover those people we wanted to see are gone. And those things we wanted to do don't matter. And the place we're going is, of all things, a gathering of God's people. Just what we thought we didn't need.

Let me confess something here: I have gone to church services (not to mention chapels, retreats and other kinds of gatherings too numerous to mention) for more than a few decades now. And, frankly, I don't always like them. Why? Because I'm just like everyone else. I have particular tastes in music, certain things I like in speakers and a particular theological bent on things. And sometimes, what I taste when I come to church . . . well, it tastes a little flat to me. Or sour. Or downright bad.

And so what do I do? Well, I begin shopping. In my mind, at least, I begin thinking about what could be. You know, we live in a wonderful time as far as worship services are concerned, because we have such a rich multitude of options available to us these days. We can go to churches of every variety and stripe you can imagine. But all this variety comes with a great danger, and the danger is that we can very easily become "worship junkies"—consumers of worship, who shop around for the most satisfying worship experience and only go to those places that make us feel the way we want to feel.

But worship is not about how I feel, first and foremost. Indeed, it isn't about me at all. Worship directs us not to ourselves but to the Other; to the Lord of heaven and earth; "to him who sits on the throne," who created everything "in heaven and on earth and under the earth and on the sea, and all that is in them"; to him who sustains all things, who is our beginning and our end; to "the Lamb, who was slain"; to the one who is "worthy . . . to receive power and wealth and wisdom and strength and honor and glory and praise" (Revelation 5).

Can you imagine having an audience with a king or a queen—think of the greatest monarchs of all times (King David, perhaps, or Julius Caesar or Queen Elizabeth)—can you imagine yourself coming to their throne, bowing before them, talking with them, listening to their advice and then walking away from the event and thinking only about yourself? Whether you had a good experience? Whether you were adequately entertained? Of course not. It's absurd. How much more absurd, then, to enter into the presence of the King of Kings through worship and do precisely that.

What are we doing when we gather together to worship our God? Precisely what my friend Gerry is doing right now in heaven with all the saints. Precisely what we will be doing for all eternity with deep gratitude and great, great joy. Like now, it won't be optional. Unlike now, we won't care. Because then we will know what we should already know right now: we do it for Him, knowing full well that for this we were created.

We *need* to gather together to worship this King. That's the point. We need it, not to escape reality, but to find it. Not to avoid the world out there, but to keep our heads screwed on straight about whose world it is. And to whom we belong. Forever.

12

ON peace & treasures
(Why Can't I Get What I Want,
When I Want it?)

When Diana Spencer —known to most as Princess Diana or Lady Di—was killed in a car accident in Paris, France, in 1997, the event captivated the world. Millions watched her funeral. And many more digested every word that flowed from the press, radio and television. It was a modern event in every sense. And it consumed us.

Her death was indeed a tragedy. And it tugged at my heart, as it always does, whenever I open the paper and learn of someone prematurely cut down through accident or crime or stupidity. Nevertheless, I have to tell you, I was struck by the extraordinary outpouring of interest, and even affection, for a person whose public accomplishments were by any standard rather modest. In saying this, I do not intend to be at all demeaning, by the way. Diana may have been a very fine person. She apparently gave herself to a number of worthy causes and, especially in her later years, seemed to reach out to those in need. Moreover, "public accomplishments," as I'm using the term, are not necessarily the highest or greatest good. Diana may have been a good sister, a good friend, a good mother perhaps. And in the long run, those qualities may have more lasting significance.

But here's the problem: Only a few people knew her as a friend. And fewer still knew her as a mother or sister. That Diana was praised and mourned by those who knew her makes infinite sense to me. The part that mystifies me, however, is the praise and interest of the rest of us—those of us who knew her *not* and had only her public accomplishments to consider. What was the basis of our interest? What was the justification for our praise?

The answer, of course, is that we all *felt* as though we knew her. We had followed the events of her life for some time, and so we were interested in her death. I use the word *felt* with purpose here, because, of course, we did not know her. We had all been exposed to snapshots of her life, her persona, filtered through the media, and that made her a public figure. But we knew her like we know all public people—almost not at all. And that makes my question all the more tantalizing: In the absence of documented or extraordinary accomplishments as well as reliable information about her life, why were we so interested in Diana's death?

Some commentators have suggested that we were interested in Diana simply because we were interested in her. She was famous merely because she was famous. She had a title with no meaning; a public life without any public purpose. But the person the media created her to be satisfied our collective need for entertainment. So the question is not, "Why did the media create Diana?" We know the answer to that: They created her and kept her alive in our eyes because we bought everything about her that they came up with. It was our consumption that fed the media. Turn off our interest and the media starves. But the media did not starve with Diana around. It grew fat and strong. And lethal.

There is some truth in that, but I worry that it overly demonizes the press and, more importantly, gets the rest of us off the hook. I don't say that in defense of the media, by the way. Their role in both creating and destroying Diana seems fairly substantial. But I think there is much more going on here. And I think it is going on in us. The real question is, "Why did we care so much about Diana? Why this interest in a person about whom we knew so little and who realized such modest public accomplishments?"

What We Want
Well, let me throw out a hypothesis: I think Diana was, and is, everything we think we want to be. Consider the following: She had wealth she didn't have to earn. Doesn't that sound great? Sort of like winning the lottery. Lots of cash. No sweat. Just fortune—an unbelievably lucky break.

She also had nobility, rank, title—that is, she had a position without power. And doesn't that sound rather fine—people bowing to you, envying you, giving you access to absolutely anything and everything you want but not expecting you to accomplish a thing because your title is honorific. Everyone knows you don't have power in your position, so you're off the hook. What could be better than that?

Diana also had popularity and fame without responsibility. She didn't have to cut another album to stay popular, score another touchdown, win another war, write another book or do any of the other things that the rest of us have to do to stay in the public eye and win our reputations. All she had to do to remain popular and famous was just . . . be Diana. And just "being Diana" made her the most photographed person in the world.

Of course, she possessed a great many other attributes we crave, including beauty, charm and grace, all of which complemented nicely the figurehead role she assumed. Quite a deal, don't you think? It's every kid's dream, in a way, wrapped up in one beautiful life.

And yet it all seemed to run amuck. Why? Why would this charmed life that represented the fulfillment of our wildest childhood dreams be so difficult, so unhappy, so full of disappointment and pain? Well, I'm no Solomon. But a few thoughts do come to mind.

To begin with, *unearned wealth* is rarely appreciated by those who have it and always envied by those who do not. And *position without power* is usually frustrating to those who hold it and seems rather silly to everyone else—not to mention meaningless, purposeless and empty. And *popularity for the sake of popularity* only breeds more popularity. Which requires more coverage, more exposure, more paparazzi. And less and less freedom. And so, surprise of surprises, what one ends up with is nothing like fulfillment or contentment, but rather jealousy, frustration, silliness and the slow but inevitable loss of one's self. Loss of one's own time. Loss of one's direction. Loss of one's identity. In short, loss of one's life.

Does that remind you of anything? Does it ring any bells? Is that not precisely (again) Adam and Eve seeking something that looks good and promises fulfillment but winds up stripping away nearly everything that truly is good? For the sake of one piece of fruit, they lost the whole garden. If nothing else, evil at its core is deception, with sin its consequence. And one of the most surprising things about us human beings is that, over and over and over again, we choose and aspire to gain those things that will inevitably destroy us.

And then, right in the midst of our grieving for Diana, we wake up one morning, open the newspapers, and suddenly learn that Mother Teresa has died as well. I think that was one of the most amazing "coincidences" of my lifetime. If any of us had written a script in which Princess Diana was killed in a car accident while being chased by paparazzi, her chauffeur having been on multiple hallucinogens, followed by the death of Mother Teresa a few days later, well . . . who would have believed it? Or produced it? We would have been laughed right off the stage. "Unreal!" people would have said. "Fantastic!" "A cosmic joke!"

But it did happen, announced in bold headlines for the entire world to see. And it was no joke. You know, sometimes we complain that God speaks too softly. That he doesn't answer our questions. That we wrestle night and day with the weighty issues of life, crying out to him, but getting no answer. Well, this time he answered. This time he hit us over the head with a two-by-four. But were we paying enough attention to know what the question was?

What We *Don't* Want

You see, if Diana was everything we think we want to be, Mother Teresa was everything we try to avoid. Like the plague. While Diana gained wealth without effort, Mother Teresa gave away what little she earned through hard work. She used her effort to lose wealth, you might say. While Diana enjoyed position without power, Mother Teresa wound up gaining enormous power without position: power based on what she gave, not what had been given to her. And while Diana was awarded status without responsibility, Mother Teresa assumed responsibility for those who had even less status than she did. Of course in the end, Mother Teresa became famous herself. But it was incidental. It hardly seemed to matter. And it did absolutely nothing to thwart her work, her character or her personal satisfaction. In fact, rather than devouring her freedom to live the life of service she chose, it enhanced her work—furthered it, expanded it, created more opportunities for it to flourish.

Of course, we admire Mother Teresa, and that makes us feel as though we identify with her objectives, which in turn makes us feel good about ourselves. But the fact is, almost everything Mother Teresa wound up getting we could have too. Who of us cannot give away our money? Who of us cannot give of our time and energy to serve the sick and the poor? Who of us cannot take on the responsibility of serving those in need?

So here's the deal: Although we admire Mother Teresa, we do not emulate her. And that makes our admiration ring a bit hollow, don't you think? We pity poor Diana. And yet we dream at night about achieving precisely what she achieved, in precisely the same way, at the same cost. Even though it cost her life.

In the end, Diana seemed to us a victim. We felt sorry for her. We were angered by those who brought her down. Mother Teresa was not a victim, however, and we felt nothing but joy and gratitude for the life she lived. She was not brought down. She was lifted up by the One who always lifts us up.

Jim Elliot, who lost his life taking the gospel to the Auca Indians, once said: "He is no fool who gives what he cannot keep to gain what he cannot lose." And that makes most of us precisely fools, I think. Dreaming of acquiring what we aren't likely to get. And what wouldn't satisfy us for more than a moment even if we did.

Why don't we get what we want when we want it? That's the question. And it's not an unfamiliar one, is it? Certainly it's a question I hear a lot in one form or another. And I have to be honest with you, it's a question I have asked myself. From day one. Indeed, I can't remember a time when I didn't ask that question. And it still periodically comes to my mind, if not to my lips.

I am a college president. That's my job. And while there is a certain mystery about what a college president actually does these days, I can tell you one thing a president does, almost all the time: try to accomplish things. Indeed, this president is nearly consumed with accomplishing things. I have my goals for the year, my objectives for the month, my daily list of things to do. And by and large, I think these objectives are worthy. But worthy or no, there's one thing I can absolutely guarantee: Some of my objectives will be thwarted. And all too often, as far as I'm concerned, the thwarted goals will be those that matter the most, the ones I *really* want to accomplish. The ones I believe will make the most difference—to the college, the faculty, the student body or to me.

And what do I do when this happens? I do the same thing everyone else does—I get ticked off. I grumble around for a while. Make nasty comments to those around me—especially those I really care about. And eventually, after I've pretty much made a fool of myself and hurt a lot of people I love, I cry out, "Why not, Lord? What are you doing, anyway? Don't you know how helpful this would be? What a good thing this would be? How much this would benefit the college? Not to mention me?"

And then, after a deep breath and a heavy sigh, I usually try to make peace with the situation by quickly—much too quickly—explaining it all away through some reference to the Fall, blaming it all on sin and saying that it's a hard life. And of course, that's all true. Life is hard. Sin is pervasive. But it never makes me feel much better. And even beyond my feelings, it doesn't seem to be a very good answer either.

The truth, however, is that most of the time I am frustrated in my dreams and aspirations not because the world is rotten, but because the Lord is good. Not because of the Fall, but because of redemption. Not because God is silent, but because he is caring and knowledgeable, and because he knows that much of what I want wouldn't be good for me. That what I desire is, in fact, not what I should have.

You see, when we say, "The Lord is good," we are typically thinking in terms of what God gives us, aren't we? Maybe it's a job. Or a love. Or a recognition. And we attribute those triumphs to God's goodness, which it may be. But I suspect that many times God's goodness is revealed not in what he gives us, but in what he withholds from us—frustrating our aspirations. And in our very frustration lies his mercy.

What We Have in Store

Remember the words of Jesus in Matthew 6:19-21: "Do not store up for yourselves treasures on earth, where moth and rust destroy, and where thieves break in and steal. But store up for yourselves treasures in heaven, where moth and rust do not destroy, and where thieves do not break in and steal. For where your treasure is, there your heart will be also."

Two things interest me most about these words of Jesus. The first is how we read them, or how we hear them. Most of us hear them as negative, don't we? "Oh dear, I've got to pursue things that only have value sometime in the future, when I get to heaven, and I shouldn't value anything now that would just be fun." But in fact, Jesus' command is very existential. He is talking about right now. *Right now,* if your goal is to amass riches, beauty and fame, right now you will pay the price. *Right now* it will be stolen. *Right now* it will fade away. *Right now* it will not satisfy or give you peace. But if your goals are those with eternal value and significance, *right now* you will have your treasure.

The second thing that interests me in this passage is the last sentence: "For where your treasure is, there your heart will be also." Jesus did not say your heart will dictate where your treasure lies, but your treasure will determine what path your heart takes. In other words, what you *do,* what you *acquire,* what you *gain,* how you *spend your time* determines how you feel, what you think about, what preoccupies or even consumes you. Your actions are the master of your attitude, not vice versa.

That lesson flew right past me when I was five years old. What I wanted was a big, red fire engine—the kind you could sit in, drive around like a tricycle, and make go "ding-ding-ding" as you hurtled down the road driving everyone around you completely crazy. And I knew that when I got that fire engine, I would be *so* happy.

It escaped me again when I was in junior high and I wanted to go to the movies instead of having to watch them on TV. For some reason my church had concluded that watching movies on television was okay, but seeing them in the theater was sinful. And so I knew there must be something wonderful and exciting about going to the movie theater. And it would make me *so* happy.

I still didn't grasp it when I went off to high school. What I wanted more than anything in the world at that time was my driver's license. I couldn't wait for the day when I could jump into a car, turn the key and go anywhere and everywhere I wanted with whomever I wanted at any time I wanted. My freedom would be unlimited, my opportunities unbelievable. And I would be *so* happy.

And I evaded it again when I graduated from high school and longed for my own car. Not just any car. I wanted a new car.

A fast car. A really cool car, with tuck and roll leather interior, glass pipes and a deep metallic paint job. I wanted a GTO! And I knew, for sure, that that would make me *so* happy.

So what happened? Well, believe it or not, in every one of these cases I got exactly what my heart desired. I got that red fire engine at the age of five, drove it around the yard for three days in a row without stopping, and then didn't touch it again for the rest of my life. Why? It was slower than my tricycle, my brother made fun of it, and the bell started driving me crazy along with everyone else.

And the movie theater? Well, eventually I managed to sneak off to the movies by myself, while no one was looking. I chose a really juicy movie called *The Days of Wine and Roses*, staring Jack Lemmon and Lee Remick, because I knew it would satisfy my every longing. And if you've seen the movie, you know what I got instead—essentially, a lecture on the dangers of alcohol abuse tucked into a haunting love story of two people torn between their love for each other and their love for the bottle. I was looking for sin, and I got a sermon.

And of course I eventually got my driver's license and, unbelievably, a brand new GTO, made to order precisely according to the dream: green metallic paint job, white tuck and roll interior, and fast—you can't believe how fast that little car could go. And what happened to the GTO? Well, it wound up being totaled, the victim of a head-on collision on California's famous Highway 1 and bearing an uncanny resemblance to a crumpled up Mercedes in Paris, France.

What happened anyway? Where did the happiness go? What became of all my childhood dreams? You see, the problem with all these things that promised to be so delightful and fulfilling was that they were not *ultimately* fulfilling. Not *designed* to produce happiness. And not designed to be forever. The biggest problem with such things, in other words, is that they are at best temporary. Quickly lost. Easily forgotten. And quite capable of being suddenly transformed into a heap of useless junk. In Paris. Or California.

Why did Jesus say, "Do not store up for yourselves treasures on earth" (Matthew 6:19)? Not because there is something wrong with material possessions, but something unworthy. They aren't bad; they just don't deserve your heart. Sometimes people read these words of Jesus and conclude that they've got to cut themselves off from material things: eat boring food, wear worn-out clothes and deny their senses. But, you know, I think that completely misses the point. Indeed, they may be every bit as trapped by materialism as those who crave it, only in reverse. Because whether you indulge yourself or cut yourself off, you are still giving things too much attention. Too much importance. Too much of your heart.

The real question is not, "Why can't I get what I want when I want it," but "To whom does my heart belong?" Jesus thinks the answer is pretty clear. Our hearts do not belong to material possessions. Or to achievements. Or to those we might want to impress. Or even to ourselves. Our hearts belong to God. Who created all things and gives us all things. Not so that we might worship the *creation*. Or despise it. But so that we might honor the *Creator* and enjoy him forever.

13

on peace & contentment

(Whine Tasting)

Why are there so many whiners in my life, anyway?" said a friend in exasperation one day. "I can't stand whiners. People need to suck it up, get real and get on with life. That's my advice. You've got to *deal,*" he said emphatically.

I considered pointing out that he was whining about whiners, but resisted the urge. I thought he had a point, after all. Whining is a major preoccupation these days. Few of us seem to think anything is actually our fault anymore, do we? If we're in debt we whine about the high cost of living. If we get a speeding ticket we whine about police traps. If the smog is bad we whine about lack of pollution controls; if it's not, we whine about the cost of fuel. And I could go on and on. Because, in our culture we have thrown off the cloak of personal responsibility and dressed ourselves in victims' clothing, turning whining into an art form in the process.

Anyway, my friend's complaint about whiners that day got me thinking about my own behavior the day before. That was a Sunday, and I was trying to get a few things done before Monday descended and the week began. Now Sunday is a day of rest, which means that I got up early so I could attend the first service at church, which would allow me to get to the garden store before the rush, to buy some fertilizer so I could fertilize the lawn before the heat of the day, and then have some time to pay the bills, after which I'd be able to finish the chapel talk I was going to give the next day before I rushed off to get pizza so we didn't have to cook but instead could spend some quality time together as a family while watching the news on CNN!

As you can tell, it was a day of rest. And it put me in a foul mood. As a result, I did what I always do when I'm in a bad mood: I snapped at people—particularly my daughter. Unfortunately for her, she had failed to put away some of her things. And she'd left a few drawers open. And she hadn't cleaned her bird cage. You know, all those things on which the totality of world history hinges.

And so I really let her have it. I told her how irresponsibly she was behaving. How disappointed I was in her. How she would probably grow up drinking wine out of a brown paper bag and sleeping on a beach somewhere. I mean, I was really something. And of course, inside I was thinking, "How could this have happened when I've lectured her a hundred times about these things? Doesn't she care? Doesn't she listen to me? Do I have even an ounce of respect left in this house?"

Well, needless to say, I had completely lost it—lost all perspective, all wisdom. And more to the point, I was whining. Big time. Whining to my family and to myself. And I must tell you, at the time, it all seemed perfectly justifiable and made tons of sense. I didn't think I was whining; I thought I was dishing out justice, being a responsible parent, reclaiming the beachhead of righteousness from the Huns of sloth and irresponsibility.

So here's the question: How do we know the difference between whining and simply telling it like it is? How do we distinguish between conclusions that are justifiable and those that are merely a product of circumstances or tiredness or low blood sugar?

Why We Whine

When she was growing up, one of our children was almost entirely predictable purely on the basis of the amount of food in her stomach. If she was hungry, she was grouchy; if she was full, she was happy as a clam and all was right with the world. And this didn't just affect her mood; it also affected her conclusions about facts. A perfectly straightforward question from me like "Honey, have you finished your homework yet?" got a completely different answer depending on the amount of food in her stomach. If she was full she'd say, "Not quite yet, Dad. Math is going a little slowly tonight. Can you give me some help?" But if she happened to be hungry, well . . . all bets were off. "Yes! I'm done! Why did you ask!" Or, "No! I'm not done! I'll never be done! I'll be doing math until the second coming! There is no way that any teacher in her right mind would assign this much material for one night!"

Now this is very interesting, don't you think? A simple question from a loving dad gets an entirely different answer, with different factual content, simply based on the amount of protein in a child's system. Can this be? Well, yes, it can be. And I'll bet if you're honest you can identify with my daughter—or with me when I lost it on Sunday during my day of "rest." You know what I'm talking about, right? Our circumstances and our physical condition seem to have enormous influence not on just how we feel, but on how we understand reality, interpret "what is," make decisions and act on them.

But now let me introduce one more piece of information into each of these stories, and I'll start with the one about me. At some point during that Sunday afternoon, when I was ranting and raving at my daughter about not cleaning her bird cage, I heard the doorbell ring. Still fuming, I marched to the front door, opened it up, and there stood the chancellor of my college and his wife, both looking as charming as ever. "Hi Stan," they said with glowing and gracious smiles. "It's such a beautiful day, we were just wondering if you and Judy would be interested in taking a walk along the beach."

"What a lovely idea," I said, smiling broadly for the first time in twenty-four hours. I invited them in and gave my wife the good news, and in short order we were all walking along the beach together having a grand time, chatting away about all kinds of things, drinking in the beauty of God's creation, and enjoying the gracious company of good friends. In a matter of minutes, in other words, everything changed: my mood, my Sunday, my view of life. Why?

Or, let's revisit my daughter's contest with math and the state of her stomach. Remember, she was hungry, she was doing her math homework, and her gentle father innocently asked how it was going. Well, in the middle of lamenting that her life was coming to an end, that the world was falling apart, and that she would never smile again . . . the telephone rang. Judy answered it and announced, "Honey, it's Will on the phone; can you talk with him now?" And then, as if a magic wand had been waved, my daughter's countenance was transformed. She practically danced to the phone to pick up the receiver. "Hi, Willy. How are you?" she said with all the charm of royalty, quickly closing the door in my face and entering an entirely different world.

"What happened?" I asked myself, still standing in the hall with the door two inches from my face. What happened, in a matter of seconds, to my daughter's disposition? And what happened to me when our friends arrived and asked us to take a walk on the beach? And why?

Note that neither my, nor my daughter's, physiology had changed one bit when the doorbell and phone rang in those situations. We maintained our same blood sugar levels. Had the same amount of food in our stomachs. But the particular circumstances that caused us to whine and complain were neutralized. They became irrelevant. In a split second, something more important to each of us had overridden our senses and rearranged our priorities. And transformed our feelings in the process.

That fact is worth noting when we ask the question about whining. Why do we whine, anyway? Well, let me put it in a positive light: We whine because we care about justice, about fairness. There is a very fine line between the whiner and the prophet. Think of John the Baptist decrying the behavior of Herod. Think about the Old Testament prophets complaining about the behavior of the children of Israel, lamenting the sins of a nation. Or think about Jesus himself lashing out at the Pharisees, rebuking them for their hypocrisy and self-righteous legalism. Aren't these complaints? You bet. Don't these sound something like whining? Indeed they do. And yet we don't think of them in those terms, do we? Why not?

Good question. Compare those complaints, for example, to my daughter's whining about her math homework. She was feeling abused and unfairly treated. Her teacher had given her more homework than she deemed reasonable. She couldn't finish it. She was going to lose sleep or get a bad grade because of her teacher's unreasonable requirement. In other words, the situation was unfair from her perspective. She was a victim, and so she issued a loud complaint.

So what's the difference—why do we think my daughter is a whiner, not a prophet? Why didn't Judy and I take her hand, march to the principal's office and demand the teacher's resignation? Well, two reasons come to mind. First, we doubted her credibility. As her parents, we knew that her complaint about math had more to do with her stomach than the math assignment. We'd seen this before; we were pretty sure we knew what was happening. But second, she was issuing the complaint on her own behalf. She's was saying, "Woe is me," not "Woe is Israel," and that made a big difference. One of the key features of an authentic whine is that it not only lacks credibility, but it is also delivered on behalf of oneself. It is *self*-serving more than justice serving.

All of this may sound pretty trivial, or even hair-splitting (I mean, who cares about an authentic whine, anyway?), unless you are the whiner. And the whine is not about homework or children, but reputation—the opinion others have of you, both now and in the future. Make no mistake, whining can be serious business. So how do we know whether our complaints on our own behalf are justified? Whether we're being prophetic or just whining?

The answer, I suspect, has something to do with *shalom,* and the state of one's heart and mind. And what strikes me is the great distance that exists between whining and shalom—between the state of your heart and mind when you're in the midst of a complaint, on the one hand, and the "peace that passes understanding" on the other. There is no peace for the whiner, is there? Indeed, while whining is pretty painful for those who have to listen to it, it is nothing compared to the turmoil in the heart of the whiner. One thing I know for sure:

When *I* am in the midst of a serious whine, it is certainly not well with my soul. *Peace like a river* is nowhere in sight.

The difference between the whiner and the prophet, then, is not only the truth of the matter—it is also the soul of the complainer. Think for just a moment about the speech that Martin Luther King Jr., delivered in Washington, D.C., not too long before his death. Most of us have seen it replayed on TV a number of times. It was his "I have a dream" speech, which stirred a nation. In some ways, that speech was a complaint. It was a complaint about prejudice. And the one delivering the complaint was also a victim of such injustice. At one level, then, you might say it was a self-serving complaint. A whine, if you will.

But there are two things that strike me about that speech as I play it over and over in my mind. First, it was not *fundamentally* a complaint, it was fundamentally a hope—a hope for a nation that included everyone. A hope that one day King's children—and all children in America—would be judged by the "content of their character, not the color of their skin." And second, I am struck by the eyes of the man delivering the speech. Check it out of the video store sometime. Replay that scene, and look at the man's eyes as he delivers that speech. You will see a man at peace. Why? Because, in his own words, he had "been to the mountaintop." He knew who was going to win in the long run. He knew what was right. He knew that what he was saying was absolutely basic to any fifth-grade education in America. And therefore he could rest in that knowledge.

Moses also was at peace when he complained to Pharaoh about the enslavement of his people and told the king to let them go. But the disciples were not when they argued over which of them would sit at Jesus' right and left in heaven. Jesus was at peace when he questioned how long he would have to put up with this "faithless and perverted generation" and then proceeded to cast out a demon from a young boy. But Judas was not when he complained about Mary's having "wasted" her costly perfume to wash Jesus' feet. John the Baptist was at peace when he lost his head, his life, for speaking the truth to King Herod.

And we will be as well—if our hearts and minds are at rest in God's shalom. Then our complaints will not be aimed simply at making everything wonderful in our private world, but directed toward bringing about righteousness and truth in the world at large. Shalom for our neighbors as much as for ourselves.

Real Peace

The peace that God gives us "passes all understanding," by the way, because it's almost always a surprise. You wouldn't predict it. It doesn't depend on circumstances, and it isn't affected by them. And it certainly doesn't hinge on our physiology. It's a peace that is quite literally out of this world, because it is God-given and centered in the soul.

Remember my daughter's peace? It came from a full stomach or a call from a friend. And it was as temporary and changeable as the circumstances of the day—precisely like her father's peace, which came from a few friends and an escape on a sandy beach. One person in our family is different, however, and that person is my wife. The rest of us are big time complainers, and we've spent years perfecting our craft. But in the eye of this storm stands Judy. Who acts rather than reacts. Who is grateful rather than resentful. And who gives thanks on a daily basis for every little thing.

And we don't understand her! She's a complete mystery to us! We try, certainly. Sometimes when we're all home together, we sit around the dinner table just trying to figure Mom out. Why in the world is she happy all the time? Why does she always see the silver lining in every dark cloud? Where does she get all her energy? How come she's always thinking about other people, rather than herself? Why is she so content? Why does she attend to her daily chores with joy and worry not a lick about the future?

And we don't have a clue! But I'll tell you what: We love it. We depend on it. And daily learn from her what life could be like—should be like—if we lived our lives differently. In other words, hers is a peace that passes understanding—ours, certainly—and we are grateful.

Not that Judy doesn't have every reason to whine and complain and feel a victim. The home she grew up in was not an easy one. She lost her father to polio when she was three, only a year or so before the first polio vaccine was introduced. Her mother then proceeded to raise two children alone, going back to school to get a teaching credential so she could teach third grade and pay the bills. On a teacher's salary. That wouldn't be easy today. It was almost impossible then.

But she did it and did it well. And through the middle of it, she had this little child, named Judy, whom she called her "little sunshine." And how important do you think that was for Judy's mom, going through the loss of her husband and partner and having her financial world turned upside down at the same time? Well, all I can tell you is that whenever she talked about her "little sunshine," her eyes danced with delight and gratitude and joy. Sort of like the way mine do when I talk about my wife, and the sunshine she has been for me and our family.

So why in the world do we so often choose whining over peace, complaint over contentment? If complaining rots the soul and poisons those around us, why do we do it? Well, there's a mystery there, I must confess. But from what I can tell, it has something to do with what matters. What really, really matters.

Willy mattered more to my daughter than an empty stomach. My friends mattered more to me than a messy bird cage. Obedience to God mattered more to Moses than Pharaoh's power. Justice mattered more to Dr. King than an easy life. Eternity mattered more to Paul and Silas than earthly chains or prison.

And do you know what matters the most to my wife? The little things brought by each new day. Doing what's right, today. Caring for those she meets on the way, today. Enjoying whatever comes her way today—from sunsets to people to a good joke to a good book. She leaves the big picture in God's hands, and the fruit of her faith and of her faithfulness is peace—*shalom*—both for herself and for those whose lives she touches.

So what about you? And what about me? Are we whiners, or are we at peace? Do we complain about what we don't have, like the children of Israel in the desert, or do we enjoy the contentment of Paul and Silas, even in prison?

On that question hangs not just how we will feel, but how we will live. And the effect we will have on those around us.

14

ON PEACE & DECISIONS
(Finding God's Will)

What now, Lord? What do I do now?" A pretty simple question, to be sure. Yet it must be a fairly important one as well, because we ask it all the time. And in a variety of different ways.

I remember one time in particular when that question seemed especially prominent. And perplexing. Judy and I had been married for about three years at the time, and we had both completed graduate programs at a university in Southern California. The question was, "Where should we go next?"—or more accurately, "Where should I go next?" since Judy was ready to start a teaching career and begin making a contribution to society. I, on the other hand, was not so interested in making a contribution. I was becoming a sociologist, after all. We don't make contributions to society, we just study it. And my hope was that I would be able to continue my studies in a Ph.D. program.

So here was the issue: I had been accepted at two universities with two very different kinds of graduate programs. One was at a university in Southern California, and the other was back east.

The eastern university had the better program, as far as I was concerned, but it was also a long way from friends and family. That wouldn't normally have been a big deal, since both Judy and I liked to travel. But about the time that we had to decide where to go, we found out that Judy was pregnant.

This, of course, was not entirely Judy's fault. But it made our decision much more difficult, because it meant that we would soon have many more financial and personal responsibilities to attend to. So the question was whether we should stay in Southern California where there were plenty of friends and family around to help us through our impending ordeal. Or should we move back east, despite the family to come, just because the program there seemed better suited to my needs?

It was a most perplexing question. And we wrestled with it for days on end, trying to figure out precisely what the Lord had in mind. Despite our efforts, however, we could find no peace. If on Monday the wind seemed to be blowing us east, on Tuesday it would blow us in exactly the opposite direction. And regardless of what conclusion we reached on Wednesday, on Thursday it wouldn't make a lick of sense. Of course, we prayed about the matter long and hard, but from the Lord we received not a smidgen of help. The silence from heaven was deafening.

All of our struggling came to a head in Fort Smith, Arkansas. Why? Well, Fort Smith is right on the route that takes you from the southwest to the southeast. And, yes, Judy and I had decided to make the big move, not because we had any great sense that it was right, but . . . well . . . because we didn't have much sense, period. We had to decide something. So we loaded our U-Haul truck to the gills, hitched our VW van behind and headed east.

Road Trip
By the time we pulled off the freeway at Fort Smith we were pretty

tired. Tired of trying to figure out the Lord's will. But physically exhausted as well, since, attempting to save money, we had only made one prolonged stop up to that point in the trip, that being an eight hour sleepover in Albuquerque. So it was a relief to be heading down a two-lane road straight for the bright lights of Fort Smith, straight for the most comfortable motel in town.

Not long before we crossed the city limits, however, I began to notice something peculiar in my rear view mirror. It was a vehicle, not terribly noteworthy except in one respect: It maintained a discrete distance between itself and our truck. That was unusual for a number of reasons. First, people don't like to follow trucks. They either speed around them, or, if that's not possible, they fall back and let the truck move on ahead. The driver of this vehicle didn't do either. He just sat there about twenty-five yards behind my truck and maintained his position perfectly. I mean perfectly.

This continued for a couple of miles and, not being a particularly patient man on the highway anyway, I began to get annoyed. "What in the world is wrong with him?" I said to myself. I was too tired to come up with an answer, so I decided just to get rid of the problem. Slowly, I began taking my foot off the accelerator, letting my speed fall back to fifty, then forty-five, now forty, and eventually down to thirty-five miles per hour. Follower didn't miss a beat, maintaining his distance with just as much precision as before. So I hit the gas, bringing my speed up to nearly seventy, but Follower remained undeterred, keeping his place a safe twenty-five yards behind.

"What the honk is he doing?" I blurted out to my sleepy wife. She paid no attention, assuming I was just in another one of my combat moods on the highway. I got my answer quickly, however, for when we finally crossed the city limits, the streetlights brought Follower into clear relief. As I peered into my rear view mirror, the thing first took the shape of a car. Then I saw it was a blue car. Then a blue car with a light on its roof. And finally a blue car with three sets of lights on its roof, a large, hatted man at its wheel, a shotgun on its dashboard, and probably a bazooka and fifteen hand grenades on its front seat. It was, in other words, a Fort Smith police car.

"Honey, we've got trouble," I said in greatly exaggerated tones.

"I know, Stan, I'm sleepy too. Just take the first motel that comes along."

"I'm not tired anymore, Judy. We've got a policeman following us and he's been tailing me for at least five miles. I don't know what the problem is, but he's definitely not a friendly."

Judy snapped to attention. "There's a motel, Stan. Let's pull in there." I obeyed, even though the place looked like a cross between a stable and a house of ill repute. As I popped out of the truck and walked to the office, I passed by a "NO VACANCY" sign but found that hard to believe. "How could a place like this be full?" I asked myself incredulously.

The man inside confirmed the message on the sign, however. "Sorry, Son, we're full up tonight," he bellowed. "Big convention in town." Again I found that hard to believe. "What kind of convention would choose a place like this?" I wondered as I made my way back to the truck. My tiredness was starting to show, along with my middle class ethnocentrism. "No luck," I said to Judy as I slumped back into the truck. "We'll have to find something a little pricier, I'm afraid."

As we headed back onto the road, I took a quick peek in my rear view mirror, assuming we had ditched the policeman but checking just to make sure. I was relieved to find that the spot twenty-five yards to our rear was now vacant. Only one car was behind us, and he was directly on our tail, no doubt anxious to get around us.

I pulled far to the right so he could pass us easily. Nothing happened. I thought it might help if I slowed down a bit, but that didn't have any effect either. I reached out the window and adjusted my mirror so that I could get a better look at the car.

"Judy," I said in a controlled scream, "Blue Bayou is still on our tail!" Judy kept her mouth shut, trying to be a calming influence and at the same time find another motel. "We haven't done anything wrong, Stan. I don't think you ought to worry about it."

"Don't worry?" I blurted out. "My dear wife, it's past midnight. We're in Arkansas, we've got California license plates, we're pulling a Hippie Wagon, and Shotgun Sally is on our tail. And you say, 'Don't worry!' What is that supposed to mean, anyway? Let's face it, we're in trouble!"

As is usual during such outbursts, Judy paid absolutely no attention to what I was saying, knowing that it would soon pass and knowing that my mouth had once again far outpaced my brain. "There's a Holiday Inn, Stan," she finally said. "Over there. Just around the corner." "Praise the Lord," I said to myself. "Middle-class America! Regular people. Regular rooms. And regular prices." The important thing, however, was that we were finally on our own turf, in a world we understood, in a world that was safe.

The sense of security did not last long, however, for again we were confronted by a "NO VACANCY" sign and a man who said, "Sorry, Son. We're full up." It was nice to know that I had so many fathers in Arkansas, but otherwise the words were not very comforting.

"Are you sure you don't have anything at all?" I asked pleadingly. "We're very tired and we've just got to find a place to stay."

"I'm sorry, young man. Convention in town. We don't have a thing."

A Moment of Truth

I must have looked crestfallen, because the man quickly followed up his assertion with a qualification. "Unless . . . unless your name is Rothen. I have a room reserved for a couple named Rothen and they haven't shown up yet. You wouldn't happen to be them, would you?" he asked with a funny sort of smile.

"I'm afraid not," I moaned as I started back for the door.

"Are you sure you're not the Rothens?" he asked more firmly, his voice following me as I continued down the hall. "If you are, I can give you a room. No questions asked."

I started to bark out an incredulous "No!" when I finally realized what he was doing. He had a room that the Rothens had reserved for the night. But it was almost one in the morning, and chances were great that the Rothens weren't going to show up. He couldn't give the room to me since the Rothens had already paid for it, but if I said I was Mr. Rothen, he was in the clear, regardless of what happened.

It was a nice gesture, and I could see by his smile that he was hoping I would go along with it. And once I realized what he was saying, there wasn't anything in the world that I wanted to do more than say, "Yes." I was tired. My nerves were shot. The world outside was a foreign land to me, full of dangers and evils that I could only imagine. And here, in this Holiday Inn, there was peace and comfort and rest. With every bone in my body, I wanted to say, "Yes, indeed. I am Mr. Rothen."

But there was another voice in my being with another answer, imprinted long ago—by a parent and then a Sunday school teacher and then by my own eyes in the quiet of my room. "Do not be deceitful" were the clear words of this voice. And their message was not at all ambiguous, nor were the implications difficult to figure out.

"Uh . . . thanks. Thanks very much," I said in the kindest

tones I could muster. "But I can't do that. I'm not Mr. Rothen . . .
though I certainly wish I were. I'll see what we can find down
the road."

"You won't find anything," the man responded quickly. "It's a
weekend night with a convention in town. I doubt there's any
vacancy within a twenty-mile radius of Fort Smith. I've got a
room, Mr. Rothen. If you'll just sign here, it's yours."

"So easy," I thought. "This would be so easy. And maybe even
right as well. After all, it's dangerous to drive while you're tired.
I've got a pregnant wife to think about. Is it right to put her at
risk on the road? Isn't a little lie here really the lesser of two
evils? Wouldn't the Lord understand?"

"Get thee behind me, Satan," I mumbled as I walked toward
the door, my mind still buzzing with possibilities.

"What's that?" the man at the counter asked.

"Oh, nothing," I said with raised voice. "I was talking to
someone else. Thanks for your help."

As I walked back to the truck, I felt tired, confused and helpless all at the same time. "Maybe this trip was a colossal mistake," I thought to myself. "Maybe the Lord really wanted us to
stay in California after all." One thing was for certain: Circumstances were not giving me any comfort. I was becoming dis-
couraged and more than a little worried. I decided to put as
much distance as possible between us and Fort Smith—and the
sooner the better. In a matter of moments, then, we were back
on the freeway, heading east once more.

It wasn't long, however, before tiredness overtook me again,
and I began wondering whether I would ever get any sleep. Fortunately, what Fort Smith lacked in the way of available lodging,
the rest of Arkansas made up for in the way of beautiful road-
side parks. And so we decided just to pull into one of them and
rest for the night. We were towing our van, after all. Why not just

get out our sleeping bags, throw them in the back of the van and catch a few winks? Well, that seemed like a perfectly good idea until we tried to put it into practice, at which time we were confronted by another Arkansas summer specialty—heat. Soggy heat. Thick, soggy heat. Traveling along at seventy miles per hour, I hadn't noticed the humidity—or the fact that the air was almost perfectly still. Lying down in our van, however, it suddenly became evident that the night was warm. The air was thick. And breezes were nonexistent.

"Hmmm . . . this isn't so good, is it Hon?" I got no response. Judy was already asleep. "Well," I thought, "maybe I can just tough it out." But as I lay there, the beads of perspiration became more pronounced and a tinge of claustrophobia descended down my spine. I knew I was doomed.

In a desperate search for relief, I jumped out of the van, threw my sleeping bag on the grass and collapsed vulnerably to the ground. Shuffling around to find a comfortable spot, I was only faintly aware of a rustling noise somewhere over my head. As the sound grew louder, I started to take heart. "'Tis the gentle stirring of a summer breeze," thought I, and I eagerly awaited the first wafts to collide gloriously with my body.

Unfortunately, it wasn't a southern breeze but a southern mosquito that descended from the heavens. And it was accompanied by an entire squadron of mosquitoes, each one fully equipped with all the appropriate armaments. Caught off guard, I began to beat my body wildly in an attempt to eliminate a few of the marauders. The mosquitoes accepted that as a challenge, however, emboldened no doubt by the fact that they were two hundred million in number and I, a mere mortal, was equipped with only two scrawny hands, both of which spent most of their time flapping harmlessly in the air.

"What kind of a place is this, anyway?" I yelled, as I rummaged through the truck looking for some mosquito spray. "These guys are vicious!"

It wasn't long before it dawned on me that I didn't have any mosquito spray and didn't even believe in the stuff. But I wanted to believe, I can tell you that. In fact, at that moment, what I wanted to do was spray the entire country with mosquito repellent. I was without means, however, so I did the next best thing. I grabbed my sleeping bag, opened the rear door of the van, announced decidedly, "We're off!" and roared once more onto the freeway, this time not stopping until we reached our final destination another ten hours down the road.

It was a *horrible* trip, to say the least, and somewhere in the midst of it—somewhere in the bowels of Fort Smith, I think—I became absolutely convinced that it was all a mistake. That we had made the wrong decision. That the Lord had really wanted us to stay in California. And that we had moved outside his will.

But then a funny thing happened. Within a few months, it became abundantly clear that not only had we *not* made a mistake, but we had made a *wonderful* decision—one of the best of our lives.

I should have figured that out right after we left Fort Smith, before we even got out of Arkansas. Since it turned out that Blue Bayou—the policeman who followed us around all over town that day—wasn't stalking us, he was guarding us. What I didn't tell you before is that, just as we were heading out of Fort Smith, he pulled us over and politely informed us that we had a tail light out on our truck. He just wanted to make sure we made it through town without incident.

I didn't believe him at the time—I was too deep in my own pity party (not to mention prejudice) to believe anything but the worst. But given what happened after we arrived at our destination, I think he was probably telling the truth. In fact, I think he was a gift from God, to be perfectly honest. As was the university program that I entered, right after we arrived, which turned out to suit my needs far better than I ever imagined it would; I couldn't have enrolled in a better graduate program. And the same thing happened to Judy. Almost immediately upon our arrival, she landed a teaching job in a nearby school system—in spite of the fact that she was pregnant and would need to take maternity leave—because they were in desperate need for someone with her skills and background. And right off the bat we found some very special friends (from Arkansas, no less!), who remain good friends to this day. I could go on and on. But the point is that, for all our difficulty both prior to and during the trip, the destination turned out to be a grand one. As much evidence of God's blessing as I have ever known in my life.

That fact, however, only served to make the whole matter of the Lord's will even more perplexing in my mind. Because, you see, now it turned out that it was not only difficult to know the Lord's will *before* you made a decision, it was difficult to figure it out even *after* a decision had been made. For weeks after we decided to move back east—and especially during those days on the road—I was absolutely convinced that we had made the wrong decision. Why? Because we were having a rotten time. The circumstances suggested that we had blown it. But we had not blown it. The circumstances were wrong. They were not a harbinger of things to come. And the picture of the future they foreshadowed did not come true.

What God's Will Is

So then, how in the world can we know the Lord's will? How do we figure it out if we can't even take our cues from our circumstances? We got a clue, the day after Fort Smith, when Judy and I found ourselves meandering aimlessly down a narrow country road full of hills and empty of people, charming and rough all at the same time. It was Arkansas at its best. And I was beginning to love it.

"Stop the truck!" Judy yelled out suddenly. Not having paid much attention to the road, I assumed we were heading for an accident, so I slammed on the brakes—hard. Whatever else one might say about U-Haul trucks, their brakes are excellent. And within a few seconds, our truck had come to a screeching halt, and Judy and I were licking dust off the front window.

"What is it, Honey?" I asked, not being able to see what the problem was and not being able to articulate a longer sentence with window grime stuck to my tongue.

"Over there, Stan. Look up on the side of that hill."

I peered out the window, expecting to see a flying saucer or the president of the United States. What I saw instead was a small but perfectly average-looking cemetery nestled among the trees about halfway up the hill.

"This is amazing, Judy! It's a cemetery! How could I have lived if I had missed this spectacle? In fact, this is worth dying for, don't you think? Let's get out of the van and erect a monument to this moment. We'll call it, 'The Moment We Almost Killed Ourselves in Order to Look at a Cemetery' monument. And all of history will be changed because of this experience. Our children will make a pilgrimage here annually, just so they can remember—

"Stan," Judy interrupted, "you are missing something. Look about one hundred yards to the right of the cemetery, a little further up the hill."

At first I couldn't see what she was talking about, but as I kept looking I noticed movement a short distance from the cemetery. As I continued scanning to the right, the full picture began to take shape. Beside the well-kept cemetery there was another graveyard, not nearly as beautiful as the first and not nearly as well maintained. The graves were marked by stones standing in irreverent postures, and the grasses beside them were scraggly and unmown. Winding up the hill to the unkempt cemetery was a small dirt path, and striding slowly within its borders was an old man, cane in one hand and flowers in the other. He was very feeble. Very determined. And very black.

We watched, spellbound now, as the man continued up the trail and finally reached an unmarked plot of grass. He stood there quietly, bowed his head for a moment, and then suddenly dropped to his knees. The drop was quick and startling, and it made us aware of our own obtrusive involvement in the scene. The man had come to spend time with a loved one and his God, not with two California transplants in a U-Haul truck. He deserved more from us than staring eyes and inquisitive minds. He deserved our absence.

I put the U-Haul in first gear and carefully began to pick up speed. The truck seemed noisier than normal, perhaps because we were trying for silence, perhaps because we were silent ourselves. Judy was the first to disturb the peace.

"What have we done?" she asked, "And why?" Her voice was quivering, weak and strong and wondering all at the same time. I knew from her tone that she was talking about history, not the noise of our van. It wasn't a question as much as a statement. And I wasn't sure she wanted an answer.

"Why do you say 'we,' Hon?" I asked. "We didn't build that cemetery. We weren't the ones who separated blacks from whites. I'm not sure I want to take responsibility for that. I have enough trouble taking responsibility for my own life. I'm not sure I want to take on the sins of history as well."

"You know what I mean, Stan," she continued gently. "I'm not talking about that cemetery, or just the sins of the past. I'm not even talking about whites and blacks, necessarily. I'm talking about people. Human beings. Why do we treat each other so badly?"

I thought I knew what she was driving at, but I also thought her question overlooked some important details. I was a sociologist, after all, and it seemed to me quite wrong to blame racial problems on humans in general.

"I'm not trying to excuse the people who did that," she continued, pointing back at the cemetery and talking as if she had read my mind. "But I want to know why they did it. Especially," she said, "I want to know why Christian people could have let it happen. I want to know why Christians in my hometown call their brown-skinned neighbors 'spicks' and 'greasers,' rather than neighbors. I want to know why we didn't say 'boo' to that working-class family who lived right across the hall from us last year. I want to know why there are people in our church who cheat their employer out of a day's labor or cheat their workers out of a fair wage. I want to know why we Christians do these things when the Bible says—from beginning to end—that we are to love God and love our neighbors as ourselves. That's pretty direct, isn't it? Pretty clear. So why don't we do it?"

It was stated as a question, though it was anything but. Judy knew the answer as well as I, and there was no reason whatsoever for either of us to say another word. People sin. That's the bottom line. Even people who know better. Even people like us, who have been schooled on Scripture from day one, who believe in its teaching and believe in its God. Though we believe, we don't always act. Though we know, we don't always find it easy to put that knowledge into practice. The problem is not *knowing* God's will, in other words. The problem is *doing* it.

And then, all of a sudden, the lights went on and the bells started ringing. And I knew, finally, that I had the answer to my life-long quest to know the Lord's will. "The problem is not knowing the Lord's will," I repeated to myself. "The problem is doing it."

Again and again I repeated the phrase, as the meaning of it began to sink in. "The challenge that God has put before me," I thought, "is not somehow to figure out his will at every turn, but to put into practice the will I know. What the Lord desires of me is to obey his commands, not attempt to discern commands where none exist; to live according to what has been revealed, not demand revelations for every one of life's choices; to obey his spoken word, not endlessly fret over words that have yet to be spoken."

"So simple," I thought as we continued down the road in silence. So simple, in fact, and so obviously right, that I began wondering how I could have missed it for so long. How could I have spent endless hours trying to decide between right and right and ignore the wrong I was doing all along the way? Why do I struggle to discern the Lord's will when it isn't necessary—when his will allows me the freedom of choice—yet fail to put the Lord's will into practice when it's as plain as the nose on my face?

Why? Because doing what is right is difficult. It's costly. I learned that in no uncertain terms at the Holiday Inn in Fort Smith. I didn't want to turn down that room. I wanted to sleep! I wanted to get some rest, and saying "No" to the clerk's offer that night was one of the hardest things I have ever done. But according to what I knew, it was right. It was, in other words, the Lord's will. And I really didn't like it.

But worrying about whether the Lord wants me to go back east to graduate school—that's the kind of thing I do like. Oh, its no fun to worry, that's for sure. But it's a lot easier than believing that God will take care of you regardless of what decision you make. That's the tough one. That takes faith. That means living with the unknown. That means living like a believer.

Better yet, worrying all the time about the Lord's will is a great way to cover up the fact that I have a problem—a deeply spiritual problem, which is that I really do not trust the Lord very much. When Jesus says, "Do not worry about tomorrow— your heavenly Father knows what you need," I really don't quite believe that. And so I run around doing precisely what an unbeliever does—worrying about what I shall eat and drink and wear, but dressing it up nicely with "Lord's will" language and assuaging my guilty conscience in the process.

How can one have peace of mind in the midst of difficult decisions? Well, for starters, you really have to believe that God cares for you as much as he says he does. You really have to believe that, regardless of what decisions you make, if you make them in good faith the Lord will not abandon you. That he really will go with you. That he really does number the hairs on your head. That he really does care for you and love you every bit as much as he says he does.

But that's hard to believe, isn't it? And so what do we do instead? What do I do instead? I worry about everything under the sun and ignore the clear teachings of Scripture at the same time. Instead of doing justice and loving mercy, I plead with the Lord to show me which parking space he wants me to use. And instead of walking humbly with my God—believing in my heart that he is a God who can be waited on and trusted and who is always faithful—I badger him to death with questions about his will. The answers to which I probably wouldn't understand if he told me. And which are no doubt none of my business anyway.

"And what does the LORD require of you?" asks the prophet. "To act justly and to love mercy and to walk humbly with your

God," comes the clear reply (Micah 6:8). And it comes to us not as advice but as a command. And it results not in a question-free life but in a peaceful heart. A heart that knows not only its beginning but its end, not only its duty but its limits. A heart that can rest in peace.

15

ON peace & wHOLLyness

*(How Can I Get Some Balance
in My Life?)*

What is the most significant problem we face as a culture?
Huge question. Easy answer. Let me explain.

When I was a senior in high school, I suspect that I was pretty
much like every other red-blooded, seventeen-year-old American high school senior of my time. If you want to get a mental
picture, just think of *American Graffiti* and you've pretty much got
my world in a snapshot. Same clothes. Same cars. Same driving
up and down Main Street from one drive-in to the next. Showing off, being cool and, let's face it, looking really, really stupid.

One Saturday night I drove into town to attend a Youth For
Christ rally. Now, YFC rallies weren't on the "cool" end of the
"cool" spectrum, of course, but they were okay. One could usually count on a funny gag or two, and it was a good time to scope
out the other . . . well, the other appropriately gendered pubes-
cents from other schools in town. But on this particular night
they not only had a speaker who was a great comedian, but he

also presented the gospel with a warmth and joy that was absolutely contagious. I distinctly remember being as moved as I have ever been by the claims of Christ and the call to follow him. And I answered that call in my heart. I was already a believer at the time, but my heart was "strangely warmed" that night, to use a good Wesleyan term, and I wanted to follow Jesus.

Which I did—for about the next ten minutes. I kept it up, certainly, as I walked out of the building. I even hung in there, still following Jesus, when I got into my car with my friends and headed onto Main Street. But somewhere before we got to Stan's Drive-In, Jesus took a right turn and I hung a left, and I suddenly found myself following someone else. In a red Corvette, if I remember correctly. With long blond hair.

Now, I'm going to resist detailing the remaining events of the night. But you should know that I committed no great sin that evening, following the red Corvette with the long blond hair and all. But I did soon find myself in a completely different environment, with a different set of people who had different values and expectations and a completely different way of thinking about things. Different, that is, from what I experienced at the YFC meeting.

In other words, in a matter of moments I was not only not following Jesus anymore, but I was transported into a completely different world. One minute the gospel was warming my heart, and ten minutes later, my heart was being warmed by something very different. Different music. Different agenda. Different hopes and dreams. I don't think any onlooker would have said it was a shift from good to evil, by the way. I wasn't doing anything obviously bad. But in my mind, what I was doing following the red Corvette with the long blond hair was absolutely unrelated—completely irrelevant—to what I had been doing at the YFC rally ten minutes before. The two events were totally disconnected. It was as though I had gone from one universe to another and become a completely different person. And here's the point: I didn't care. I did not care.

Now why am I telling you this story? Because I think what happened to me that night is exactly what happens to all of us in this culture all the time. We are all regularly transported from one setting to the next, each with entirely different values and expectations. We may not go from YFC rallies to drive-ins anymore, but think of what we do on any given day—what the average student does, the average physician, the average person in sales or management or services or anything else.

The Dis-integrated Life

Take your average college student, at an average university in America, for an average day. You wake up to the music of your favorite radio station, take a shower and hang out for a few minutes with friends. Then you go to your first class—biology— where the professor happens to be a Christian and sees the whole world as a magnificent piece of art resulting from the hand of the Creator. You leave class, walk over to the cafeteria, get in line, and you suddenly think of the whole world as something to eat, to devour and to consume. You then go to a history class, this time taught by a Marxist, and the whole world is transformed into a class struggle in which the rich exploit the poor. Then you go back to your room, surf the net for a little diversion, and are now transported into absolutely any world you want—at any place, with any person, talking about anything from gardening to cooking to sports to sex.

Something you come across reminds you that you need a new shirt, so you run off to the mall and enter a whole new world of stimulation and promise loaded with things you can

buy to make you feel better or prettier or more attractive. You
return to your room to try to study, which doesn't go too well
because you keep thinking about the shirt you bought, which
doesn't look nearly as good as the one you really wanted but
couldn't afford. So you tune in to MTV for a little while and
enter another world entirely. After a quick stop at McDonald's,
you run over to the college across town, which has a vespers service that evening, and suddenly you find yourself deeply moved
in praise and adoration of God, singing your heart out in love
for him.

Vespers over, you jump back into your car and head back to
your room. On the way, you see a friend who wants to go
dancing on Main Street. Within less than an hour, you're back
in a state of ecstasy (so to speak), feeling very much like you
felt at the vespers service, but with a different purpose, a different beat and a different object of praise and adoration.
Finally, you head back home, fall into bed, put in a CD and fall
asleep. Maybe.

And here's the thing: This is not atypical. All of us in this culture go through this kind of disjointed routine practically every
day, whether we're college students, business people, stay-at-
home moms and dads, retirees—you name it. And we think
nothing of it, don't we? I mean, this is our life. This is our daily
experience. And it's not too bad, is it? Or . . . is it?

Well, think for a moment about what is happening and what's
not happening. What's happening is that, on any given day, you
and I do a whole host of things that are completely disconnected from each other, and we accept it as normal. What's *not*
happening is integrity: living life as an integrated whole centered around a common purpose, working toward a common
end and in service to a common Lord. On any given day, we
may or may not commit what we perceive as an obvious sin. But

we also live our lives for no obvious purpose, other than to be entertained and variously stimulated. And we are perfectly happy to be stimulated by Jesus on one occasion and by something else the next.

What happens then (to all of us, I would contend) is that we tend to think of Jesus not as the Lord of our life but as just one fragment of a very fragmented day. One more piece of entertainment. One more possible source of learning. Sometimes interesting, sometimes irrelevant. Sometimes moving us to tears, sometimes moving us not at all. And so our hearts are warmed by Jesus at one moment and warmed by something else the next. And we hardly even notice. Or care.

Now this is a problem for one obvious reason: Jesus is not "something else." He is the beginning and the end, the one in whom are hidden all the treasures of wisdom and knowledge. This is how John describes Jesus as he launches his Gospel: "In the beginning was the Word, and the Word was with God, and the Word was God. He was with God in the beginning. Through him all things were made; without him nothing was made that has been made. In him was life, and that life was the light of men." And then, a few verses later, to drive it home: "The Word became flesh and made his dwelling among us. We have seen his glory, the glory of the One and Only, who came from the Father, full of grace and truth" (verses 1-4, 14).

So here's the question: "What does that mean for us, regardless of whether we're at home or work or play?" What it means is that there is nothing—absolutely nothing—that is disconnected from Jesus. The word "Irrelevant" does not apply. And it doesn't matter whether we acknowledge that fact or not, or understand it or not, or believe it or not. The whole world belongs to him, was created through him and will find its end in him.

That being the case, then every one of those moments in our lives when we think he is irrelevant is a fiction. It's a lie. It means that regardless of what we are doing or when we are doing it, if we do not think of our lives—at that moment—as being connected to our faith . . . well, we are wrong. Which means that, in this culture, we're wrong a lot. It means that we are a people without wholeness, without integrity, without direction, without peace.

Beyond the Balanced Life

So what do we do about it? Good question. And a popular answer these days is "Balance." A while ago I was talking to a friend—who happens to be a scholar—who was complaining to me about the lack of balance in his life. He said he was working too hard and needed to kick back, think less, enjoy life more and get his discipline out of his head once in a while. Now I know what he was saying; at least at one level he was saying he shouldn't be so serious all the time, that he needed to lighten up. And perhaps he had a point. But at another level he was quite wrong. We don't need more balance in our lives, if balance means doing a large number of things that are disconnected from each other and disconnected from our Lord.

Indeed, I think that idea from a biblical perspective is quite bizarre. Can you imagine Jesus saying to his disciples, "Okay guys, here's the deal. We need a little balance in our lives, so why don't we follow Beelzebub today. And then, Judas, perhaps you can be Lord tomorrow. And then, on Tuesday, if you don't mind, I'd like to be Lord again. Just for a time, you understand. Just to keep our lives balanced."

That's absurd, of course. But I think for many of us that's exactly what balance means: it means giving Jesus a little piece of the action, a little part of our day, but making sure we have some time to ourselves as well so we don't get too stressed out. But it doesn't work because it just multiplies the number of things we have to get done in a day's time. That kind of balance doesn't decrease stress, it increases it. What we need is not balance, but wholeness. It is *shalom,* the peace that comes from reconciliation, from being rightly related to God, to one another and to God's creation. It is our lives as a whole finding meaning and purpose and direction in our Creator.

And that does not mean being serious all the time, by the way. Laughter is every bit as much a gift as contemplation. But it *does* mean being *available* all the time—in our laughter and tears, our joys and sorrows, our dancing and embracing, our reading and writing, our speaking and listening, our playing and serving—in all things that God gives us and knows that we need. It means being available to God's Spirit to teach us, to grow us and to enable us to be the people God created us to be in the first place. It means following Christ in all things, at all times, in all directions. It means when the red Corvette takes a left turn and Jesus takes a right, going right.

But still, how do I do that? How do I follow Christ—in my work, in my relationships, in my family, in my free time—in such a way that it all hangs together, so the parts become a whole? Good question. But the wrong question, assuming one wants an answer. Indeed, what is required for this journey is not certainty about the details, but availability for the trip.

Several years ago, I kept in touch with a student who was taking advantage of one of our study-abroad programs. During the year, we conversed via e-mail, so I was able to learn about his adventures on an almost weekly basis. The year turned out to be a very stretching experience for him, both personally and academically, and somewhere right in the middle of it (while he was in Italy, actually), it all came together for him. His study of

literature and philosophy suddenly dovetailed with his appreci-
ation for art and history and theology. And he was pretty much
dumbstruck—overwhelmed by the sheer magnificence of it all.

At about the same time, he also found himself thinking about
himself. Who he was. Where he was going. Why he was going
there. And with whom. In other words, he was experiencing
"senioritis"—having senior thoughts, wondering about his
future. But what struck me as we e-mailed back and forth was
not the details of his thinking but his conclusions.

"Today, I found myself surrounded by some of the most
beautiful art the world has ever known," he observed. "And
somewhere, right in the middle of it, I found myself praying.
But it was different from how I have prayed in the past. Today I
prayed with my palms up, asking God to fill them as he wanted
to take me where he wanted, to teach me what he wanted, and
to give me the companions, or companion, he wanted me to
have. In other words, I told the Lord this morning that I'm
available, that I want to be his student."

"Palms up," I thought to myself. That's it. Not a brilliant conclusion about the nature of Renaissance art. Not a sudden realization that he should become an artist himself or a pastor or a
professor. Not some flash of insight about whom he should
marry or where he should live or even how. Just "palms up."
What he wanted more than anything else was to learn what God
wanted him to learn. To be where God wanted him to be. And
to enjoy whatever God wanted him to enjoy.

And I think that's what it all comes down to for all of us.
Regardless of our vocation, regardless of our calling. Where is
wholeness? How do we find shalom? By being available, with
palms up. Available to learn whatever God would teach us, to go
wherever he wants to take us, to be whomever he has created us
to be, in every circumstance, in every moment. "Palms up" is not

just a warm heart; it's an open life. A heart that motivates feet to move, hands to serve and a mind to learn. Hands that, when seeing a neighbor in need, reach out to serve. Minds—those that thirst for that which is true and right and good and beautiful. And not easily satisfied.

"Palms up" is to say no to the fiction of our age, which makes life a series of fragmented, disconnected experiences, and yes to the truth of Christ, in whom we live and breathe and have our being.

16

ON peace & prosperity
(Happiness Revisited)

a few Saturdays ago we had one of those rare and wonderful mornings when we weren't feeling too pressed for time. Kirsten was already out and about, doing whatever seventeen-year-olds do on Saturday mornings (when they're not sleeping), and I was pondering what I would talk about in chapel the next week. Judy was catching up on her reading, browsing through a well-known periodical. All of the sudden she said, "Jennifer Lyon! Hey, Stan, come look at this. There's an article here about Jennifer Lyon and some new Gen-X thing she started. Did you see it?"

She handed me the magazine and I quickly scanned the article and the picture. Yep, there she was, in living color. Jennifer Lyon. Only, she isn't Jennifer Lyon anymore, according to the article. She's married now and sporting a new name. But she's Jennifer Lyon to me. And always will be. Now the significance of this is that Jennifer is a former student of mine, who managed to orchestrate one of the more interesting moments of my life: a breakfast at the White House with the president of the United States, which included a private tour of the White House along with the West Wing offices, and a chance to chat with the president and vice president. And again, it was all because of Jennifer Lyon.

Now the interesting thing is that Jennifer pulled this off only a year after she graduated from college. And she did it by becoming a nanny. Well, that's not quite right. But it's not entirely wrong either. You see, Jennifer was a good student. Bright and visionary. And during her junior year, she participated in an internship program in Washington, D.C. A complicated set of circumstances wound up connecting her with Phil and Linda Lader, who had two young daughters and a very interesting life. Phil Lader was the deputy chief of staff at the White House at the time. And Linda was one of the president's volunteer religious liaisons and the president of the Renaissance Weekends. Impressed with Jennifer, they asked her to live with them immediately after graduation, both to help care for their daughters and to assist Linda, especially in the development of these Renaissance Weekends. Which she did. With joy and extraordinary success.

One of her first duties, it turns out, was to help Linda put together a breakfast at the White House with the president and a few religious leaders from across the nation. As they were putting the invitation list together Jennifer said, "I think you should invite Dr. Gaede." Linda said, "Who's he?" Jennifer then went on to invent all kinds of nice things to say about me and handed her a copy of my latest book. Linda pretended to like the book. And I got invited to the White House for breakfast.

Stepping Out
But that's not the best part of the story. The best part of the story

is Jennifer, who quickly emerged as a key player in the development of these Renaissance Weekends. Then she fell in love, got married and quickly became a key player in putting together a good marriage. And then she took a position at the Coalition for Christian Colleges and Universities where she got the idea of a Renaissance Weekend for Christians in their twenties and thirties. She has now become a key player in putting together the Vine, a yearly retreat for emerging Christian leaders in all walks of life and from all denominations who want to worship together, share their struggles and triumphs, and imagine what they might do together as followers of Christ at this moment in the life of our nation.

And here's the best part: It's exactly the same kind of imagining that Jennifer was doing while sitting in my office as a twenty-year-old college junior some ten years ago now. Exactly. And she had no idea what to do with it. None. All she knew, at the time, was that she loved the Lord a lot. Loved him with heart, mind, soul and strength, to use the biblical language. She knew as well that Christ loved his church and wanted his people to work together, not apart. But she also knew that too often we Christians live fairly fragmented lives these days, each doing our own thing—rarely living our lives as integrated people, much less participating in an integrated community of faith. And, finally, she knew it shouldn't be that way. And with that fairly limited knowledge, she stepped out. She stepped out, and she stepped into a blazing furnace.

Jennifer wasn't the first to do that, of course. In fact, Jennifer's story reminds me of two other students in different circumstances but with similar hearts. The first is John Davidson, currently a distinguished professor at one of the finest universities in the nation. He is in academic circles what would be called a success story. But he didn't start out that way.

In fact, as an undergraduate John was probably known more for his soccer skills and clever wit than for his academic prowess. But at some point during his junior year he suddenly became very serious about certain questions, the most fundamental being what is wrong with our culture and what should we being doing about it? That sounds very abstract, I know, but for him it was almost palpable. As a Christian, he cared about his neighbor. And he thought too many of his neighbors, both Christian and otherwise, were in trouble. And he wondered why. And that took him on a quest, which was—in my experience, anyway—rather unusual. Two examples.

During his senior year, John came to my office one day and asked me if I would give him and a few of his friends a tutorial covering the life and thought of Jacques Ellul. Ellul is a French Christian and social critic, who writes broadly on almost anything, but especially political, social and religious topics. I don't always agree with him, and he's not an easy read—especially not his social thought. But John found him intriguing and wanted to learn more. So I agreed to set up a separate seminar on Ellul. We would read one book a week, meet to discuss it and then they would write papers in response. The workload was ridiculous—for them and for me—but they hung in there. And I've never taught a more exciting class in all my life.

The second unusual thing he did was to take six months right after he graduated from college and travel throughout Asia. On his own. This wasn't for fun, in other words. This was for learning. He didn't think he could understand his own culture until he experienced others. And so he took this solo journey throughout Southeast Asia, kept a journal and returned home. More troubled than ever, I might add. But also more determined than ever to figure out what was wrong in our culture and what was right, and what his faith in Christ was calling him to do as a result. And that turned out to be graduate school, first of all. And after that, the world of scholarship where he has encountered extraordinary success. But not before he stepped out—and stepped into a blazing furnace.

Which leads me to a third student, by the name of Andrew Raymond, who graduated about ten years after John. Andrew was perhaps the brightest student I have ever encountered in my life. He was number one in his class and could have majored in math, economics, theology or sociology. He chose the latter almost by lot but continued taking courses in the other three just for fun. Like Jennifer and John, Andrew was a delightful fellow who loved to laugh and loved life as well. But he loved God more than anything, and he desired to be obedient to God's calling on his life, no matter where that would take him.

And as you might expect, given his grades and GREs, he thought that meant graduate school. And so he applied to the best programs in the country and was accepted everyplace he applied. He wound up at a university in the Midwest, where he received a wonderful fellowship, and began his work. Things went well academically, but spiritually he could not find peace in his work. He prayed about it, and through a long series of events, decided that he was called to be a high school teacher, not a college professor. And since you can't teach just sociology in high school, he picked up a quick credential and started teaching in an urban high school.

He loved his work this time and thought he had found his place. But within a few years, he got the opportunity to teach high school in another part of the world—can't tell you where—among a people who do not know Christ, cannot know Christ, and do not want Westerners there telling them about Christ. But that's what he's doing anyway: teaching high

school—all alone. Living for Jesus—all alone. Living like
Jesus—all alone. And answering questions about Jesus, as best
he can. And he, Andrew Raymond, is in a blazing furnace—
right now. And having the time of his life.

Facing the Flames

Then Nebuchadnezzar flew into a rage and ordered Shadrach,
Meshach, and Abednego to be brought before him. When they
were brought in Nebuchadnezzar said to them, "Is it true,
Shadrach, Meshach, and Abednego, that you refuse to serve my
gods or to worship the gold statue I have set up? I will give you
one more chance. If you bow down and worship the statue I
have made when you hear the sound of the musical instruments,
all will be well. But if you refuse, you will be thrown immediately
into the blazing furnace. What god will be able to rescue you
from my power then?

Shadrach, Meshach, and Abednego replied, "Oh Nebuchadnezzar, we do not need to defend ourselves before you. If we are
thrown into the blazing furnace, the God whom we serve is able
to save us. He will rescue us from your power, Your Majesty. But
even if he doesn't, Your Majesty can be sure that we will never
serve your gods or worship the gold statue you have set up."
(Daniel 3:13-18 NLT)

I love Andrew. He puts my faith to shame. The teacher has
become the student, and the student, the teacher. As has John.
And as has Jennifer. And they have done it—like Shadrach,
Meshach and Abednego—by saying no to Nebuchadnezzar
and yes to a blazing furnace.

But they weren't the same, these blazing furnaces that they
faced. For Jennifer, it was simply the fact of who she was: a
charming, intelligent and beautiful young woman in a culture
that prizes exactly those characteristics. And it said to her,

"Come, Jennifer, worship at the feet of pleasure and enjoyment; take up the good life and leave the abundant life behind." And Jennifer said, "Not a chance, Nebuchadnezzar. I'm following my Lord."

And then the flames began to grow hot: Why in the world are you a nanny, Jennifer? You're a college graduate. Get a real job. And what are these Renaissance Weekends anyway? Everyone knows they're just junkets allowing the political elite to schmoose with the wealthy, to hobnob with the rich. And what about your friends, Jennifer? Why would you leave them behind? Life is short. Relationships are all that matter. Why in the world are you pursuing this dream of uniting a fragmented church in a fragmented world? Talk about unrealistic, Jennifer. You're only young once, you know. Not beautiful for long, you know.

And Jennifer's response? "O Culture, I do not need to defend myself before you. If I am thrown into the blazing furnace of an unknown future, the God whom I serve is able to save me. He will rescue me from your power. But even if he doesn't, O Culture, you can be sure that I will never serve your gods or worship the values you have set up."

And Jennifer walked into the furnace and through the fire unscathed. Wound up finding exactly the people and project she needed to pursue her vision. A dream in process, being realized, one might say. But not until she walked into the fire, not knowing when she walked in if she would survive. But knowing in her soul that it didn't matter. Because what the culture required was unconscionable. And what her God offered, instead, was incomparable.

Oh, I love Jennifer. And I love John as well, who also walked into the furnace, by the way, when he walked into graduate school. You'll recall that John went on a hunt after graduation,

186 An Incomplete Guide

looking for some answers and pursuing them around the world. Once home, he knew only a couple of things: whom he should marry and whom he should follow. And that took him to graduate school, where he encountered colleagues and fellow graduate students who believed and lived differently from how he did. They thought his perspective was off, as well as his life. And this wasn't just your average "You may be wrong about that, John" experience. This was the blazing furnace which threatened his integrity, his success in graduate school and his future as a scholar.

And why was that? Because John had come to some very unpopular conclusions about the sources of our culture's difficulties. Conclusions that were thought to be anathema by most other scholars in his discipline at that time. Nevertheless, he argued his conclusions without embarrassment and without flinching. And that was costly. Costly in terms of friends and relationships at times. But costly, perhaps, for his future success as a scholar as well. Indeed, because of these conclusions, everything he dreamed of pursuing was on the line.

And what was his response? "O Discipline, I do not need to defend myself before you. If I am thrown into the blazing furnace of academic disgrace or failure, the God whom I serve is able to save me. He will rescue me from your power, your majesty. But even if he doesn't, O Discipline, you can be sure that I will never serve your gods or worship the values you have set up."

And the fire hurt. And continues to singe at points. But God has been faithful, and John has prospered, in spite of the heat. Indeed, from a human perspective, John wound up at the top of the heap. Vindicated by others in his discipline. And widely honored for his work within the academy. But, you see, the honor doesn't matter because it comes from the same people that threw him into the fire in the first place. And its value is the

same, whether it takes the form of a reward or a threat. And
John knows that. And it shows.

And I love John. As I love Andrew. Who is still very much in
the fire, by the way. But what I didn't tell you, is how he got
there. You'll recall that Andrew is the smartest person I've ever
met, who gave up one academic career to pursue another,
becoming an inner-city high school teacher, then a resident in
another part of the globe where he continues to teach and
share Jesus, but does so in a place where Jesus is not particularly welcome. That, in itself, might be considered a furnace to
most people.

But here's the part I didn't tell you: Andrew, you'll recall, is
pretty much doing this all alone. And while he doesn't mind
silence, he also loves people. And friends. And Andrew needs
encouragement, just like the rest of us. And most of all, Andrew
would love to be married someday. And have a family. But the
road he has chosen makes that almost impossible. In fact,
makes a life of isolation and loneliness almost inevitable. No
one around who shares his faith. No one around who shares
his dreams and aspirations. And no one around with whom to
share his life. That's a given.

And the world says, "What in blazes are you doing, Andrew
Raymond? You only live once. Why in the world are you wasting
it in a foreign land? You will get no converts, you know. You will
have no friends who really understand you, you know. You will
have no life, you know. No life. No wife. No family. No future."

And Andrew says, "O World, I do not need to defend myself
before you. If I am thrown into the blazing furnace of isolation
and loneliness, the God whom I serve is able to save me. He will
rescue me from your power. But even if he doesn't, O World,
you can be sure that I will never serve your gods or worship the
values you have set up."

And the blaze continues. And Andrew? Well, I think Andrew
is having the time of his life. He is growing to love the people
whom God has now given him, for one thing. But his love for
God and his relationship with God have never been deeper or
fuller. I have never seen him more confident, more at ease,
more at peace than he is right now. Right now. In the midst of
fire.

The Pursuit of Real Happiness
I love Andrew. And I love Jennifer. And I love John. And I don't
mean that I love them in the generic sense, like one loves all
people. I mean that their lives and how they have chosen to live
them warms my heart. And it does so not because of who they
are but for what they've done with what God has given them.
You see, these were ordinary people in many ways. Oh, one was
pretty bright and one was good at soccer and one was fairly out-
going. But they all had their failings as well. People who liked
them and people who didn't. Good ideas and dumb ideas. Good
days and bad days. Their grades varied. Their behavior varied.
Their place varied. They were normal, in other words. Normal
Christians. From normal churches. Who had accepted Christ as
their Savior in the normal way and sought to make him Lord of
their lives.
But two things marked them rather abnormally in the process. The first was a longing deep in their being that they didn't
entirely understand, but which they could not and would not
ignore. It was a longing for something more than what their
world had to offer. Something more, something bigger and
something better. They did not despise the world; indeed, they
rather enjoyed it. But they were realistic as well. And they knew
that what they longed for wasn't available in the things dished
up by our culture. And they faced up to that fact early. When

they woke up with a hangover or a failed romance or a failed ambition they didn't say, "Whoops, better luck next time." They said, "Not enough. Not good enough!" They saw the world for what it was, in other words, and longed for something better.

Which brings me to the second unusual thing about them: When they figured out the point of their longing, they had the wisdom and the chutzpah to reorder their lives around it, come hell or high water. They let go of that which didn't satisfy, in other words, to pursue that which did. Which is why when they came to the blazing furnace they went through it, not around it. Which is why when they were told to worship the gods of our age—whether success or popularity or acceptance or whatever—they all said, "No, thank you." Just like Shadrach, Meshach and Abednego.

And why did they do this? Shadrach, Meshach and Abednego? Jennifer, John and Andrew? What was this thing they longed for which, when they found it, made all other ambitions pale in significance? Well, you might say they just wanted a little peace and happiness. But that wouldn't be quite right. Because they wanted a lot of peace and happiness. Not for a moment, but forever. Not as a future promise, but as a present reality.

And what they debunked in the process is one of the great lies of our age (and sometimes we even get this in church, so we're talking real deception here). The lie is that *loving God* is about some future happiness, giving up satisfaction now for future bliss. While *loving the world* is about trading away the future for pure enjoyment now. But the truth is precisely the reverse. And in our saner moments we all know that.

Name one worldly pleasure that you have ever experienced that measures up to the promise. Name one. Sex. Money. Power. Adulation. Respect. Fill in the blank. Oh, we talk to each other as if they're great. And we'll laugh and share stories about our feats and convince ourselves how amazing they are. But eventually, our friends will leave. The lights will go off. And we will be left alone. And then we will know what we should have known all along: that neither you nor I have ever in our lives found any of those things either to be very satisfying, nor in retrospect all that magnificent. It is only their future promise that keeps us going. The promise that, next time, it really will be worth it. That if we just have a little bit more it will finally be enough. And it never is. Never is.

Which means that the person who lives his or her life for the future, in fantasyland, is not the one who loves God, but the one who loves the world. Who lives under the illusion that pursuing the things God created can satisfy more than the One who created them.

I am sometimes asked, "What do you want most for your students?" And the answer is easy. I want them to be happy. Truly happy. Not later, but now. Not just Saturday night, but Saturday morning as well. And Sunday morning. And every morning that God gives them breath. So happy, in fact, and so at peace that when the blazing furnace comes—and it will come, by the way, guaranteed; you don't live the truth in the midst of lies without facing the furnace once in a while—when it comes they won't give it a second thought. For why would anyone trade away even one moment with our God for anything else, much less for an eternity?

Shadrach, Meshach and Abednego weren't brave, my friends. They were smart. To paraphrase Jim Elliot once again, one is no fool to give what cannot be kept and never satisfies, to gain that which cannot be lost and satisfies forever. You want peace and happiness? Remember Shadrach, Meshach and Abednego. Remember not their bravery, but their intelligence. Not their sacrifice, but their gain.

epiLogue

7th Standard

(A Road Less Traveled)

In rural areas roads are not simply means to an end—no mere conduits to the achievement of some other purpose. There aren't many of them, for one thing. One or two options to get from here to there. Maybe three. And over time you prefer one over the other. Fewer potholes, perhaps. Fewer cars, more than likely. Or just the sense that here is an old friend, whom you need to visit once in awhile.

One such old friend was 7th Standard. Can't remember how it got its name. Growing up, one accepted road names like cousins. They were there, for as long as you could remember, and one rarely questioned their legitimacy or nomenclature. What I remember quite distinctly, however, was the look and feel of 7th Standard. It was straight and true, on the one hand. Absolutely trustworthy in support and direction. But it had one rather surprising feature: a dip in the road that tickled the stomach and always brought a smile to my face. And, over time, I came to love both features.

Most people didn't travel 7th Standard. It wasn't the fastest route to town, for one thing, and it was eventually superseded by a four-lane highway that connected with a freeway. If you wanted a speedy journey, you took a different route. And if you wanted lots of options—turnoffs that could take you to multiple destinations—the freeway was clearly the way to go. A few old-timers stuck with 7th Standard, along with those who needed it to tend a farms or ranch. Or needed to visit an old friend.

The funny thing is, I can't ever remember being happy while driving down the freeway. I'm sure I was. But I can't remember it. Too preoccupied with getting home, I suspect. Or getting to the city, for that matter. But I do remember enjoying 7th Standard. A lot. All the time, in fact. Enjoying it like an old friend, who is reliable from beginning to end, and who never fails to tickle one's fancy at some point on the journey.

The thing is, you don't take 7th Standard just to get someplace in the hope of fulfilling some future promise. You take it for what it is. Right now. A good road. Good and right and true and beautiful. A road that, curiously enough, never fails to take you where you wanted to go in the first place but delivers all along the way as well.